Against the Odds: Chronicles of Resilience (Book 1)

Breaking Chains: Overcoming Systemic Barriers

Jordan B. Smith Jr. Ed. D.

© Copyright 2024 - All rights reserved.

The content contained within this book may not be reproduced, duplicated or transmitted without direct written permission from the author or the publisher.

Under no circumstances will any blame or legal responsibility be held against the publisher, or author, for any damages, reparation, or monetary loss due to the information contained within this book, either directly or indirectly.

Legal Notice:

This book is copyright protected. It is only for personal use. You cannot amend, distribute, sell, use, quote or paraphrase any part, or the content within this book, without the consent of the author or publisher.

Disclaimer Notice:

Please note the information contained within this document is for educational and entertainment purposes only. All effort has been executed to present accurate, up to date, reliable, complete information. No warranties of any kind are declared or implied. Readers acknowledge that the author is not engaged in the rendering of legal, financial, medical or professional advice. The content within this book has been derived from various sources. Please consult a licensed professional before attempting any techniques outlined in this book.

By reading this document, the reader agrees that under no circumstances is the author responsible for any losses, direct or indirect, that are incurred as a result of the use of the information contained within this document, including, but not limited to, errors, omissions, or inaccuracies.

Table of Contents

MAKING A DIFFERENCE 1

CHAPTER 1: A CHANGE IS BORN 3

CHAPTER 2: A LEAP OF FAITH 13

CHAPTER 3: THE START OF SOMETHING NEW 23

CHAPTER 4: THE THRESHOLD CROSSED 37

CHAPTER 5: THE FIRST LESSON 43

CHAPTER 6: IN THE MOONLIGHT 51

CHAPTER 7: BROKEN TRUST 57

CHAPTER 8: A GUIDING HAND 71

CHAPTER 9: ADVOCATING FOR CHANGE 77

CHAPTER 10: THE WINTER CONCERT 89

CHAPTER 11: LEADERS ARE BORN EVERY DAY 93

CHAPTER 12: CHANGE BREEDS PROGRESS 101

CHAPTER 13: OUR STRENGTH IS IN OUR SUPPORT 107

CHAPTER 14: THREE LITTLE WORDS 113

CHAPTER 15: TO FURTHER HEIGHTS 121

CHAPTER 16: THE AWARD CEREMONY 129

CHAPTER 17: GROWTH TAKES TIME 135

CHAPTER 18: AGAINST THE ODDS 143

CHAPTER 19: A PARTY PIECE OF SUCCESS 157

CHAPTER 20: THE DAWN OF A NEW ERA 165

Making a Difference

"A teacher affects eternity; he can never tell where his influence stops."

– Henry Adams

In a survey conducted by OnePoll in 2019, 83% of respondents said that they could recall a teacher who had made a meaningful impact on their life. I can certainly remember teachers who profoundly impacted me, and one, in particular, inspired me to go into teaching.

As teachers, we all want to make a difference to our students and hope to be remembered long after children move on… That, after all, is why you're reading this book – you want to do everything you can to make a positive difference to the kids you teach and help them understand the concepts they struggle with.

And the beauty of teaching in the modern world is that it's easy for us to share information and experiences, making a difference not just to the children we teach but to each other as teachers.

So, I'd like to take this opportunity to ask you a small favor.

With just a few minutes of your time, you can help me assist more teachers desperately trying to reach those students who have given up on learning.

Whether you are a veteran teacher looking to transition into a teacher leadership role or starting as a teacher looking for inspiration, this book is the perfect book to help teachers grow and become better educators.

By leaving a review of this book on Amazon, you'll help improve other teachers looking to transition into a teacher leadership role or inspire those thinking about responding to the hidden voice calling them to become teachers.

B0D433TLPM

By letting other readers know how this book has helped you and what they can expect to find inside, you'll show them where they can find the guidance they need to help the students who struggle the most.

Thank you for your support. We all want to be that one teacher that someone remembers years down the line – and when we share our resources, we can help each other get there. You can use this link:

Or Scan the QR Code to complete a review! https://qrco.de/bf3f7K

or https://www.amazon.com/review/create-review/?asin=B0D433TLPM

Add Me to Your Mailing list for a Free Copy of my next Book.

Chapter 1:

A Change is Born

Benjamin

Benjamin knew something had to change. The passion for education that once fueled his every step was faltering. The reason behind this was not because he was any less committed to his calling, but in fact exactly the opposite. He loved his students and he wanted to support them in ways that he knew the traditional education system simply could not provide, which is why he signed up for this alternative education workshop. He fervently hoped he would find the inspiration he needed to address the challenges that many of his students faced at Ridgefield High.

He had walked into that workshop with renewed hope and vigor, his steps practically bouncing as he strode into the room. He was ready to take on this challenge, even if he had to do it alone. And he fully expected to do it alone, because he knew many of his fellow educators disagreed with his controversial sentiments.

Which is why meeting Sarah caught him off guard.

The room was spacious, brightly lit, and not unlike any other meeting room; complete with a large, half-moon table that was surrounded by chairs and a Smart Board that hung on the wall in front of it where presentations could be displayed. The rest of the room was filled with a couple of smaller tables scattered about with only one or two chairs tucked underneath them, and on the left-hand wall was a small counter with a little red coffee machine alongside cheap paper cups and a dainty wicker basket full of creamers and sugar packets.

Benjamin took a seat at the large, central table, where a diverse set of educators from various backgrounds surrounded him. Some of the faces were familiar, while others were new to him. Peter Howes, a progressive board member of Ridgefield High who had earned Benjamin's respect by being a long-time advocate for alternative education, was a friendly face among the table, while one of the attendees he had not met before was seated beside him.

She had long, sandy-colored hair that cascaded in waves down her shoulders and her creamy caramel skin shone in the morning light. A notepad and fountain pen sat on the table in front of her, and she eagerly prepared to take notes as the presentation began.

A middle-aged Indian man with short-cropped black hair that was speckled with gray stood at the front of the table and coughed pointedly to direct everyone's attention.

"Good morning, my name is Naveen Patel and today I will be guiding this professional development seminar on alternative education," he said before turning to pull up a PowerPoint on the Smart Board.

"Alright, so let's start with universal public education," Naveen said as he flipped to the first slide.

I heard the woman beside me scoff under he breath as she put her pen down defiantly. "I can't believe that's what we're starting with," she muttered quietly.

Benjamin chuckled to himself, trying to be subtle but apparently failing because she turned to him with redness crawling up her cheeks. "I didn't mean to say that out loud," she admitted sheepishly.

"It's okay, I understand where you're coming from. It's not exactly the birthplace of an education system that nurtures individual growth and development."

"Right?" she agreed avidly, clearly animated by the topic.

They shared a warm smile before turning their attention back to the slideshow.

Naveen continued with his presentation, and while he definitely had some good points to share, Benjamin couldn't help but feel like it lacked the inspiration he sought.

When they took a coffee break, Benjamin was feeling slightly less hopeful than he was when he walked into the workshop, but he wasn't ready to give up just like that—he cared for his students too much to let them down.

He meandered over to the coffee counter and started fixing himself a cup, hoping the caffeine would help him re-access the knowledge he just gained from the slideshow and somehow find the catalyst he needed to provide a solution for his students. He was so lost in thought that he didn't even realize someone was beside him until a honey-sweet voice startled him from his contemplations.

"So, what do you think of the slideshow so far?"

He glanced up to see the woman who sat beside him earlier smiling up at him with a cup of coffee in her hands.

"Oh, um, it's very interesting, but to be honest I was hoping for a ground-breaking discovery that would inspire me and address the issues that my students are facing within the confining regiment of traditional schooling."

Benjamin prepared himself for the falter he was used to teachers facing him with when he shared his views on alternative education, but being at a seminar on the topic must've turned the tide because Sarah nodded enthusiastically, not missing a beat. "I completely agree, the traditional education systems we currently have in place utterly fail to address the challenges that marginalized students are forced to face."

Benjamin blinked in surprise. His years of experience with educators who were complacent with the traditional systems and had no desire whatsoever to elicit change had him not expecting such an astute response.

"I'm Sarah, by the way—Sarah Mitchell. Can I ask your name?"

"Benjamin Diamonds, I'm a math teacher at Ridgefield High."

"It's nice to meet you, Benjamin," Sarah said with a warm smile. "I must admit it's very refreshing to discuss this topic with someone who actually seems engaged by it. Do you want to sit with me? I'd love to talk more about this with you."

Benjamin had never had much luck with women so he was surprised by her unsolicited request, but he found himself drawn to the intelligence that shone in her eyes and the palpable excitement that radiated off of her. Plus, he was just as eager to converse with someone who could match his passion for education as she seemed to be.

"I could talk about this all day," he admitted with a wide grin.

They made their way over to the nearest table and sat down across from each other, where they spent the rest of the coffee break discussing the systematic failings of the traditional education system and sharing their past experiences that highlighted these shortcomings. They also eagerly discussed ideas that they believed could greatly improve the education system, especially for marginalized students.

"It's been really hard to watch my students suffer through the challenges they face without the proper support they deserve. I really care about them and I know I can do better for them, but it's difficult when you only have so many tools at your disposal and the education system is so flawed," Benjamin said as he sipped on the last dregs of his coffee.

"I know exactly what you mean, and I really believe that alternative education could solve a lot of the issues that your students have to withstand," Sarah responded earnestly.

"I think so too, but it's not as accessible as it should be for them, I wish there was a program that offered them the alternative education and support they need, but I guess that's just too much to ask." Benjamin shook his head forlornly.

Sarah was quiet for a moment, and Benjamin could practically see the gears whirring in her mind as she contemplated the issue that stood before them. After a while, she leaned forward slightly and smiled brightly, a twinkle in her eye exposing the idea that must have just formed in her head.

"What if we offered them that program?" She must have seen the surprise flash across his face because she pushed forward without waiting for a response, "I know we just met and we hardly know each other and this is a huge undertaking to even consider with a random stranger, but in this short conversation we've talked more directly about the failings of our current education system than most educators have let me to in years. You said it yourself; your students deserve better and they don't have access to a lot of options—so let's provide them with the support and alternative education that they deserve. Let's be the support they need to graduate feeling empowered, informed, and hopeful for the future they hold."

A slow smile spread across Benjamin's face as he realized something. "You know," he said slowly, smiling brightly at Sarah, "I walked into this seminar today looking for change, for a spark that would propel me toward the answer I was looking for; the answer that I needed to help my students. I thought the information from this presentation would be my catalyst, but I never would have guessed that you would walk right up to me and offer exactly the solution I need."

He leaned forward slightly too and matched her excited expression. "Sarah Mitchell, I would love to open this program with you. Let's do it."

***

The coffee break only lasted so long, and Benjamin and Sarah were nowhere near done discussing the breakthrough they just had together, so they walked to a café across the street and continued hashing out the details of their new program, from student support systems and mental health programs to innovative teaching methodologies and potential curricula.

"I can't believe how much ground we've covered already and it's only 11," Sarah said with a smile.

"I know right? It's crazy, when I woke up this morning I was still mulling over how to address my student's challenges and now here we are figuring out how to do just that." Benjamin smiled animatedly back at her.

"So what are we going to call it?" Sarah asked.

"That's a good question." Benjamin thought for a moment, his brows creased in introspection. "I want the name to symbolize all the potential it can hold for students and the places it can bring them to. Something that illustrates the new dawn it can facilitate for them."

"I think that's a great name right there: 'Diversity Dawn Academy.'"

A lopsided grin spread across Benjamin's face. "There you go again with your great ideas. I think this is the beginning of something extraordinary Sarah, and I want to thank you for being the spark that started this whole thing."

Sarah looked down at the muffin on her plate to hide the blush Benjamin could see creeping into her cheeks. "Thanks Benjamin, but you're the one who came up with it—I just pointed it out."

"You know what the next step is right?" Benjamin said as he leaned forward slightly, trying to move past the compliment that had Sarah blushing so that he didn't make her feel uncomfortable.

Sarah smiled as if she were reading his mind. "We have to pitch this to Ridgefield High."

Benjamin leaned back, smiling and wondering what he did to deserve such an amazing colleague.

***

"So you want to open a program that offers alternative education here at Ridgefield High, huh?" said Evan Peters, the Principal of the Board at Ridgefield High. He was a small Caucasian man with a bald head and a graying mustache, and he peered through his slim square glasses to raise an exceptionally furry eyebrow at Benjamin and Sarah, who were sitting in front of the five school board members.

"Yes, we believe that it can offer specialized support to individual students who are forced to face hardships based on their marginalized status, such as LGBTQ+ members and students from different ethnic backgrounds," Benjamin said confidently.

"This program could change the lives of these students, and in our modern day and age inclusivity and mental health awareness are a crucial part of life, especially for adolescents who are already navigating the complexities of transitioning from children to adults," Sarah added from her seat beside him.

Quinn Jackson, a stunningly tall middle-aged African American woman with short, tight black curls framing the top of her head, nodded with a warm smile in agreeance along with Peter Howes, but the rest of the members didn't seem entirely convinced.

"If you just give us a chance to bring this vision into a reality, I'm sure the positive ripple effect it can create will speak volumes for the undeniable change that it can facilitate," Benjamin pressed, not willing to let them dismiss the idea without fully considering it first. "Graduation rates will increase exponentially, just like they have for other schools that implemented tools drawn from alternative education models."

"Very well," Evan said as he leaned back in his chair to address them. "You have two weeks to prepare your final pitch. If you blow us away with all that the program can offer, then we will consider approving your request and backing the program."

"Thank you, you won't regret this. Diversity Dawn Academy will change the lives of those students for the better—I promise," Sarah said animatedly.

"Let's just hope that promise doesn't fall short, Ms. Mitchell."

***

Benjamin and Sarah spent the next two weeks rigorously preparing their pitch. They were both very passionate about the program and firmly believed it could be the solution to the issues that many marginalized students at Ridgefield High faced, so they poured their all into making sure that the school board had no choice but to give them a chance.

"I think that went well," Sarah said spiritedly as she walked down the steps of Bloomingdale High to catch up with Benjamin, who stood at the bottom waiting for her. They had just finished their tour of the school's alternative education program, and they could feel the subtle warmth of hope growing in their chests.

"Yeah I think so too, I was really impressed by those students—they genuinely seem to be thriving. It's so refreshing to see that after all the adversities I've had to witness my students struggle with."

Sarah nodded solemnly as they walked to Benjamin's car together. "Don't worry—we're gonna knock their socks off tomorrow with this pitch, and then we'll be one step closer to brightening your students' futures."

Benjamin smiled gratefully at her as they got into his car.

"We have plenty of insights from all three of the schools we visited with successful alternative education programs," Sarah continued, "what do you say we head back to my place and integrate these real-life examples into the proposal to make sure it's ready for the pitch tomorrow?"

Benjamin was quiet for a moment as he turned his car on. They had only ever worked together at coffee shops or the local library and going to her house seemed intimate, like their professional relationship was transcending a threshold that they hadn't crossed yet.

Don't make it weird, Benjamin thought to himself, *she's just offering because it's too late to go to a café or the library.*

Which was true; they had arrived at the school just as the students were wrapping up their last classes and the tour had lasted over an hour so the cozy Californian sun was slowly drifting closer to dipping behind the horizon of skyscrapers that formed their peripheral.

Sarah must've noticed his hesitation because she frowned imperceptibly in confusion and opened her mouth to retract her offer, but closed it as she noticed a smile spreading across Benjamin's face.

"Sure, let's do that. I don't think I can sleep tonight without making sure everything is ready for tomorrow," he admitted with a chuckle.

Sarah smiled in relief as she buckled her seatbelt. "Yeah neither could I, I'm so excited and nervous at the same time."

"Me too," Benjamin admitted as he pulled out of the school parking lot.

It turned out that Sarah's apartment wasn't too far away from Bloomingdale High, so it didn't take them long to settle on her soft red leather couch and set up their notes on the wooden coffee table in front of them.

"So we've done all our research, we've collected real-life examples, we've addressed staffing needs and budget requirements, and we've crafted answers to every potential question they may have. Do you think that's everything?" Sarah asked as she flipped through the final draft of the pitch.

"Don't forget the plans to integrate the program into the existing school structure without disrupting the current education system. I'm sure they'll bring that up," Benjamin added.

"Right, that's in here too." She shook her head and sunk back into her couch, letting the draft flop onto the coffee table. "I can't believe we have to work so hard to convince the board to back this program, it's astonishing to me that the benefits don't jump out at them like they do for us."

Benjamin nodded sadly in agreement. "Some people find change difficult, terrifying even, and they'll avoid it at all costs. I saw a lot of that during my service as a Marine; people who clung to their beliefs no matter how skewed they were because it was all they knew."

"You were a Marine?" Sarah asked, sitting up from her slouched position and raising a slender eyebrow in question.

"For a time, yes—but educating is my true passion. I would do anything to help my students access the resources and support they deserve."

"I can tell, I've never met anyone as dedicated to their field as you. It's inspiring," Sarah said earnestly.

Benjamin cleared his throat as he felt his cheeks heat in embarrassment. Receiving compliments had never been one of his strong suits.

"Thanks," he mumbled sheepishly, reaching out to pick up the pitch again. "Let's practice those answers one more time, I want to make sure I know them so well that I can recite them in my sleep."

Sarah chuckled and shifted on the couch so she could sit up straight and face him directly as she pretended to be a board member.

***

It was dark by the time they agreed that they'd done all the preparing they could and that if they kept it up they wouldn't be as well-rested as they needed to be for the pitch tomorrow. Benjamin stared up at the twinkling stars in the night sky as he stood in front of his car and reveled in the giddy feeling of excitement that seeped its way through every pore of his body. He had felt so lost just two weeks ago, and now he was trembling with exhilaration as he imagined the potential that this program could hold. It was exactly the change he was looking for, and he couldn't wait to convince the school board that it could shape a new world of informed, empowered, and resilient students—if only given a chance.

Chapter 2:

A Leap of Faith

Benjamin

Benjamin wanted to know where all the confidence he felt last night went. He was so sure of himself when he closed his eyes and drifted off to sleep, but a restless night spent worrying about the repercussions of not being able to offer his students this resource snuffed his confidence away like a flame sputtering out in the rain. He couldn't stop worrying about what would happen if the school board refused to support the program and he had to go back to helplessly watching as his students suffered silently.

Sarah seemed to notice his nervousness though, because she grasped him gently by the shoulders and offered him a bright, confident smile. "Hey, we got this, okay? We've covered all our bases and they can't ignore the facts. They're going to have to approve the program just for the potential to turn graduation rates around, never mind all the other benefits it can offer. So don't stress, okay? Just think about your students and how much they need you to be calm and collected right now."

Benjamin nodded firmly, feeling much more grounded and inspired to give this pitch his all. "Thank you, Sarah, I needed to hear that."

"No problem, we all need a little encouragement now and then." She smiled at him again and shuffled through the pitch. "Alright, let's go over this one more time before the board members arrive."

They were seated in the exact same dimly lit meeting room that they had sat in front of the board almost two weeks ago, and Benjamin could only hope that this time they wouldn't face as much hesitation as they did before.

It wasn't long before the board members started filtering in and finding their seats as the clock ticked to 7:00 a.m. They had 45 minutes to convince the board that this program was the future of education before they had to wrap the pitch up and prepare for the school day to begin.

The air became charged with tension as the board members settled into their seats, looking expectantly at Benjamin and Sarah.

"Good morning everyone, let's begin this meeting. Mr. Diamonds, Ms. Mitchell, now is your chance to convince us why we should consider facilitating this program of yours," Evan Peters said as he leveled his gaze on the two educators seated in front of him.

"Thank you Mr. Peters, and all of you for taking the time out of your day to consider this pitch," Benjamin began. "As you all know, graduation rates have plummeted in recent years as the mental health crisis becomes more and more prevalent in our modern society; spreading its dark tendrils like a devastating plague sought to drag us all down and withhold our country from reaching its true potential."

Benjamin had expected to use the notes that he had spent the last two weeks carefully crafting, but as he looked across the table full of board members in front of him and felt his chest fill with determination, he found himself speaking freely and spilling his sentiments directly from his heart in an effort to make them understand how important this program was.

"Throughout my 20 years as an educator, I have spent an exorbitant amount of time desperately trying to support countless students under my wing who have slipped through the cracks of our current education system because they face challenges such as mental health issues, LGBTQ+ discrimination, immigration hardships, and racial prejudice. With only so many tools at my disposal, I have had to stand by and watch helplessly as my students suffer through their individual adversities feeling unseen and unsupported. As educators, it is our job to provide youth with all the tools they need to face the world as confident, informed, and empowered adults—but how can we do that if our education system is hopelessly outdated and not suited to address the needs of our modern age?"

Sarah smiled proudly at him as she took the lead, just like they practiced. "Diversity Dawn Academy can fill the gaps left by the traditional education system and offer personalized student support systems for marginalized students who deserve more than we can offer them with our current resources. By focusing on their individual needs and catering to support them through the hardships they face, this alternative education model will send graduation rates through the roof and therefore foster a new age of students who look to their future with hope and purpose instead of drowning in the pit of despair that our current education system has proved helpless to save them from."

They leaned forward in their chairs together, breathless with anticipation for the board members' reaction to the hook that they had practiced relentlessly for the last two weeks.

Peter Howes was smiling and seemed whole-heartedly convinced, but Benjamin and Sarah had expected that and were more concerned with the unimpressed expressions that filled the rest of the room. Even Quinn Jackson, who had seemed prepared to support the program when they first brought it to the board, looked skeptical.

"What would the budget requirements be?" Quinn asked.

"One of the best aspects of this program is that it will not require an excessive budget allowance since it will be run through the resources that are already present here at Ridgefield High—such as utility, transportation, and custodial services. However, we will require a set number of rooms to hold classes in and propose to use portable classrooms as they are cost efficient and easy to set up," Benjamin answered smoothly, having anticipated this query. "Here is a proposed budget for the program that we prepared in advance; it covers all the details."

Quinn nodded as she took the budget from Benjamin and looked it over, seemingly satisfied with that answer and not itching to ask any other questions.

"It is extremely important that, if it were to be approved, this program does not interfere with existing classes. How do you propose to facilitate that?" George Harrison, a stout board member with a pudgy face and narrow eyes, asked pointedly.

"That's another benefit of the portable classrooms," Sarah said proudly, "they will be positioned on the school grounds and therefore separate from the classes that will be held inside the main building; avoiding the disruption of students who are not enrolled in the program."

George didn't seem convinced but he also couldn't seem to come up with a retort and instead sunk into his chair, which was struggling to hold his weight.

"And how are you going to address staffing needs?" Miriam Jenkins said. She was the fifth member of the board, and she had wrinkled white skin and gray hair pulled back in a bun that was so tight it looked uncomfortable.

"The program will require teachers for the five foundational subjects," Benjamin responded. "We propose that I should be the math teacher and integrate my current class into the program as the majority of my current students will be interested in the program, and Ms. Mitchell will be the English teacher as she is currently seeking employment and meets all the requirements. That means we will require three more educators to cover science, social studies, and PE/electives, which is included in the budget."

"I still don't see why this program is necessary," George huffed, "I think it's a waste of time and resources."

"I agree. I don't see how it can improve the graduation rates as drastically as you claim it will," Evan said curtly.

"As we explained, studies show that students drop out due to a lack of support for internal and external challenges they face and this program can address their concerns by providing individualized student support plans," Sarah said, visibly trying to remain calm and not lash out at their ignorance.

"But what about potential backlash from the community for funding a program that supports LGBTQ+ students and those who are facing immigration issues? That could potentially affect our donor contributions," Evan retorted.

Benjamin watched as Sarah's face flushed with anger and contorted in a way that suggested she was about to tell Mr. Peters exactly how disgusting it was that he was prioritizing money over the well-being of the students. His mind raced as he tried to think of a rebuttal that would dismiss his skepticism before Sarah ripped into Evan with a verbal lashing that would throw their chance of his approval down the gutter. Before he could, though, Peter Howes cut in with a strained smile.

"I highly doubt that will be an issue Evan, most of our donors are very progressive and will likely support this endeavor wholeheartedly."

Evan sank back in his seat, clearly disappointed that his bluff had been called.

"I really don't see how we can pass up this chance to increase our graduation rates," Peter continued, "especially since they're lower than they've ever been and haven't shown any sign of increasing in the last *five years*. I've seen the results of alternative education systems firsthand during my time as an educator in Europe, and believe me when I say this is exactly what Ridgefield High needs and has been missing out on for a long time.

"If we want to keep this school running, we need to cast aside our inhibitions and embrace the future with open arms—for the sake of the students. After all, isn't that why we each ventured into this profession? To provide a solid foundation for the youth of our country by supporting and empowering them? If you can't answer that question with an unwavering *yes* that shakes you to your very core, then perhaps you should wonder if you chose the right calling." Peter looked pointedly at Evan, who scowled and shrank further into his chair.

"Now," Peter continued, "who is in favor of supporting our students and providing them with the resources they deserve?"

Peter raised his own hand before he had even finished his sentence, and Quinn quickly followed suit. Even George and Miriam reluctantly raised their arms above their heads in agreeance.

Evan scowled and glared at Benjamin and Sarah but eventually sighed and said, "Fine, but I only agree on a conditional one-year approval. If the graduation rates increase as much as you claim they will, then we can reassess the long-term feasibility of the program."

"Thank you sir, however I would like to let the board know that in order to show realistic growth and impact on the graduation rate, a two-year pilot would be optimal as it will allow us to receive 11th and 12th graders instead of only those who have decreased chances of graduating without the program," Sarah said. Benjamin nodded solemnly beside her.

"All in favor of a two-year pilot?" Peter asked, glancing around at his fellow board members expectantly.

Everyone—including Evan—eventually raised their hands, although it took an unnervingly long time for the Principal of the Board to do so, almost as if he wanted to see Benjamin and Sarah squirm.

Benjamin let out a breath he hadn't realized he'd been holding and looked beside him at Sarah, who seemed just as relieved as he was. They smiled at each other proudly as they shared a look of triumph that soon intertwined with determination as the realization of what they had just taken on dawned upon them.

***

The next few days were a blur as Benjamin and Sarah dove head-first into the early stages of bringing the program to life. From ordering the portable classrooms to consulting with a construction crew about optimal placement and estimated construction time and—the lengthiest and most important task—carefully interviewing and selecting staff members that will uplift and brighten the program, they had their hands full. As busy as Benjamin was though, he never felt overwhelmed—he was much too excited for that. The main feeling he experienced was gratitude. He was grateful for the chance to be a part of a program that could really help his students, and he was especially grateful that he had Sarah by his side every step of the way.

By the end of the week, they had one last interview set up before they began considering which candidates would be chosen to fill the limited number of positions they had available. So far, most of the interviews were with people who not only shared Benjamin's and Sarah's views on the importance of the program, but were also fiercely passionate about alternative education and social justice—which was exactly what they were looking for. It was going to be hard to pick through so many promising candidates.

The last interviewee showed up exactly on time, which was one of the criteria that Benjamin and Sarah agreed was an essential skill that the potential candidates must possess—excellent time management. After all, they couldn't be showing up late for classes.

Benjamin and Sarah stood up to shake the interviewee's hand as she approached the small table where the interview would be conducted. She was short in stature and looked a little younger than most of the other interviewees but her determined, fiery brown eyes that twinkled with intelligence made her seem anything but small. She had dark, chocolate-colored skin and a tight afro that suited her face well. A warm smile spread across her full lips as she firmly shook their hands.

"Good afternoon Ms. Honey, it's a pleasure to meet you," Benjamin said as they all settled back into their seats. Benjamin and Sarah were seated on one side of the table and Beatrice Honey sat in the chair across from them.

"Your resume and cover letter were quite impressive and we've been looking forward to this interview," Sarah said as she glanced over the resume that sat before her on the table.

"Thank you, I am very grateful for a chance to showcase what a valuable addition I can make to this program. I am a firm believer in the transformative power of alternative education and I have a wealth of experience as an educator in various alternative education models. I've been looking forward to this interview as well," she said with a bright, confident smile.

"That's exactly what we're looking for," Benjamin said. "As I'm sure you know, this program is in its early stages of development and we need educators who can uplift our students and prepare them for the modern challenges that they will face when they graduate. We're carefully selecting teachers to fill the positions of science, social studies, and PE/electives. You mentioned on your application that you're applying for the science position?"

"Yes," Beatrice confirmed with a nod.

"Can you tell us a little bit more about yourself and why you believe you're a great fit for this position?" Sarah asked, looking up from the resume.

"I studied abroad and completed a Bachelor of Science at the University of Oxford, where I also interned as a TA in an alternative education program to gain hands-on experience. From there, I traveled to Africa where I spent two years facilitating an alternative education system in Ghana. I recently returned to California to reconnect with my childhood community and figure out my next steps. A friend of mine suggested I apply to this program and I jumped at the opportunity to work in an alternative education environment again. It is my fervent hope that I can be a part of this program so I can support marginalized students through the challenges they face, just like I did in Africa."

Benjamin and Sarah share an astonished look for a split second before turning back to Beatrice. "I must say, your background is very impressive. Of course, we knew all this from your resume, but it is even more inspirational when explained in person," Benjamin admitted.

Sarah nodded in agreeance. "We have just a few more questions for you to make sure your personality aligns with the program."

Beatrice's answers to every question blew them away, and by the end of the interview they had to resist the urge to hire her right then and there. Instead, they thanked her politely and told her that they would be in touch soon with a decision, but they knew the decision was already made without even communicating with each other first.

"Well at least we don't have to wonder who's going to be the science teacher," Benjamin said with a chuckle after she had left the room.

Sarah chuckled with him, her almond-shaped hazel eyes bright with excitement. "That only leaves the social studies teacher and the PE/electives teacher to choose now."

"With so many extraordinary candidates, it's going to be a tough decision," Benjamin said with a sigh.

Sarah nodded animatedly. "It sure is, which is why we better get started."

***

It took Benjamin and Sarah three days to sort through the candidates and eventually choose the educators to fill the remaining positions. When they finally did, they felt like a weight had been lifted off their chests, and they eagerly reached out to each person to tell them the good news.

Once that was done, they spent a couple days tying up loose ends and planning a small unveiling ceremony that would be held once the construction was complete and the program was ready to start its journey.

It felt like forever for Sarah and Benjamin before that day finally came.

"I want to thank you all for coming and taking the time to celebrate this special day," Benjamin said to the small crowd that stood before him. It couldn't even be called a crowd really, there were less than a dozen people present, but Benjamin had always preferred quality over quantity. He looked out across the small green hill in front of the school grounds that they had chosen to have the ceremony and saw Quinn Jackson beside Peter Howes, along with Beatrice Honey and the rest of the staff they had hired, and a couple community representatives and parents who he knew were excited about the program as well.

"I also want to thank Ms. Mitchell, the co-founder, for being the spark I needed and for all the work she's put into this program. Without you,

Sarah, we wouldn't be gathered here today," Benjamin said, glancing beside him to give Sarah a warm, proud smile.

"Diversity Dawn Academy is just that—a chance for students to start a new chapter of their life, to feel supported through the challenges they face, and to enter the workforce feeling informed, empowered, and hopeful for the future. After all, isn't that what they deserve?"

The encouraging sound of applause fills the air and Benjamin turns to Sarah, whose eyes are shimmering with hope and glistening with tears of joy. They share an emotional smile, and Benjamin knows he can overcome whatever hardships the program may face with this dynamic and innovative educator by his side.

Chapter 3:

The Start of Something New

Maria

Maria couldn't remember the last time they had a family dinner like this. No tense conversations or unspoken words, just warm, loving smiles and the delicious aroma of her *abuela's* famous *pozole* wafting through the humid evening air as they sat before their food with their heads bowed in prayer.

It was so unlike most nights at the Gonzalez's household. Most nights the air was charged with tension, and anxiety riddled the wrinkled skin of her grandparent's faces. As undocumented immigrants, the dark storm cloud of fear loomed over them constantly, which made it hard for Maria to feel comfortable in her own home. Most days she found herself developing her own storm cloud of turbulent emotions, as if the darkness could spread like a disease in the wind.

But not tonight. Tonight was oddly peaceful, as if her grandparents had found the eye of the storm and sought shelter in the tentative feeling of solace and security. She wasn't the only one who noticed it; she could practically see the weight lift from her parents' shoulders as they eased into the relaxed setting of the evening. Her younger siblings seemed more oblivious to what was going on around them, but that was nothing different from how it always was. They were just too young to be aware of such things.

Maria glanced around the worn, nostalgic wooden table that had been around for as long as she could remember and felt her heart sing with the stirrings of hope as she listened to the amiable conversations that filled the air. It seemed like the perfect night to ask the question that had been burning inside her chest since she saw the flyer outside

Ridgefield High's main office. She probably would never have a better chance than this, when everyone seemed laid back and less strict than they usually were. She swallowed her food and took a big, shaky breath; fervently hoping that they wouldn't crush her dream like she expected them to.

Before she could open her mouth to speak though, her *padre* turned his attention to her like he had sensed what she was about to ask.

"How has school been Maria?" he asked as he dabbed the grease from his lips with a napkin.

"Good, papa. I got a B in English," Maria said proudly. While that may not sound like something most students would boast about, it was much better than most of her grades. No one in her family liked to talk about the fact that the storm clouds made it hard to focus on school.

"That's great *mija*," her *madre* said with a warm smile. With luscious long black hair and ruby red lips set against golden tan skin, her mother was the picture of beauty and she always lit up the room when she smiled. Maria only hoped that her mother's smile could make everyone feel so at ease that they would actually consider her question.

"Speaking of which, since I've been doing so well in school, I was wondering if I could sign up for some extracurriculars for the next school year," Maria said nonchalantly, hoping they wouldn't pry.

"I see nothing wrong with that," her padre said, causing the tipsy feeling of hope to tingle in Maria's chest. That is, until her *abuelo* caught on to what she was saying and narrowed his eyes in suspicion.

"What would you be doing?" he asked in broken English. He always tried to practice his English whenever possible so his lack of fluency wouldn't draw attention to himself, but the love he held for his mother tongue seemed to hold him back from fully embracing the language of the country he now lived in.

Maria shifted uncomfortably in her seat and stared at her hands in her lap. Part of her wished that she hadn't opened her mouth to begin with, but the tiny kernel of hope burned warmly in her heart and urged her to answer the question. After all, if she never asked, she would never know whether they would say yes or not. So she took a deep breath and looked up into her *abuelo's* fiery hazel eyes with a flame of defiance set alight in her own.

"It's a seat in the school band, I want to play violin—and not just alone in my room."

Maria felt her hope sputter and shrink as she watched her *abuelo's* lips press into a hard line. Still, she could see the sadness in his eyes and she knew that he wished he could say yes, so she pushed on.

"I won't play very well, I promise. No one will even notice me."

The thick, wire-framed glasses that sat on top of her abuelo's head moved slightly as he shook his head adamantly.

"You know why we can't let you do that *mija,*" her *abuela* said gently, without looking into her eyes. It was true, Maria knew all too well that every single member of her family was forbidden to draw attention to themselves (whether it was good or bad attention) for fear that it may lead to her grandparents being deported, but she was so tired of living her life in constant fear and she truly believed that no harm would come from her playing in the school band.

"But I won't draw attention to myself, and even if I did why would they ask questions? My English is perfect and—"

"*Silencio*!" her *abuelo* snapped, cutting her argument into pieces. "I don't want to hear any more of this."

Maria felt hot tears form as she stood abruptly from her chair and stormed out of the room without another word.

She barged into the room she shared with her siblings and headed straight for the lonely window on the far wall, climbing out onto the only place she could find some semblance of privacy in the cramped apartment that her large family struggled to fit in—the roof.

She curled her knees up against her chest and buried her head in them, letting her tears stream freely in a silent sob for help that no one heard.

***

Maria tried to shake off the numb feeling that had settled in her bones the next day, but it clung to her like a damp shirt on a cold evening. She moved through her classes without feeling fully present, like she was looking in at her surroundings from afar through a murky plane of glass.

When the final bell rang, Maria decided to take on an extra shift at her local community center. She worked there whenever she could because money was always scarce and she usually looked forward to the rare days she had off, but today she just wanted to avoid facing the stifling feeling that awaited her at home.

When she arrived, a brightly colored flyer caught her eye from the bulletin board it was pinned on.

Diversity Dawn Academy was formatted in bold letters to look like a sun rising over a hill, and Maria found herself leaning closer to read the rest of the words on the page.

As she did, she felt the kernel of hope spark in her chest once more.

Jamal

Jamal had always found solace in his ability to write. Each stroke of his pen felt like a weight lifted off his chest as he allowed the words to flow in a stream of self-expression. He had never been a fan of writing short stories or essays, but the gentle whispers of poetry had always held him captivated and he had found a passion for it at a very young age.

Which is why his mother was encouraging him to try out for the poetry contest at Ridgefield High after he casually mentioned it to her at breakfast. With his father not in the picture for a reason that she refused to tell him, it had just been him and his mother for as long as he could remember. Because of that, and the fact that he didn't have many friends, he was closer to his mother than anyone else in his life.

"You can do it babycakes, your poetry is better than anyone else's in that damn school and you know it," his mother said as she plopped a box of cornflakes on the table in front of him.

"I don't know Ma," Jamal mumbled as he poured himself a bowl and reached for the milk jug beside him. "Even if it was, I don't really want to share it with anyone. The kids at school think I'm weird enough already."

"Oh hush, they're the ones who are weird. Your poetry is a damn gift and it ought to be shared," she said firmly, her dark amber eyes flashing with fiery determination. Jamal knew better than to argue with her—it never ended well—so he sighed heavily and stared down at his bowl of cornflakes in defeat.

It wasn't long before it was time for him to start walking to school, so he got up and brought his now empty bowl to the sink where his mother was standing and kissed her on the cheek. A flicker of a smile hinted at the corner of her mouth, and Jamal could tell that she knew she won the battle.

"Have a good day babycakes, and don't forget to think about which poem you're gonna submit for the contest," she said with a smug, loving smile as she turned to watch him leave.

"You too Ma, and okay," he said as he grabbed his backpack from where it sat beside the kitchen table and slung it over his shoulder as he pushed open the screen door.

The walk to school was always Jamal's favorite part of the day, because he wasn't surrounded by people who didn't understand him or treated him differently because of the color of his skin. He always left a little early so he didn't have to rush and could enjoy the walk without stressing about Mrs. Hampson snapping at him for being late again. It wasn't his fault that he got distracted by the hidden beauty of the world around him, it was part of why he loved poetry—because it let him express the sublimity of the world that could always be seen if one just stopped to look.

It was always over too quickly though, because before he knew it he was standing in front of the garishly outdated stone column doors of Ridgefield High and wishing he didn't have to walk through them. But he never turned around and walked away from them because he knew it would break his mother's heart. Ever since he told her that he wanted to go to the University of California, she started working tirelessly every day to tuck aside extra cash to put towards it and he knew he couldn't let her down—even if going to Ridgefield High nearly suffocated his passion for poetry and post-secondary education.

The day didn't drag by as slowly as it usually did, but that was only because Jamal wasn't ready for lunch when he would have to submit his poetry contest entry. He debated not submitting it and just telling his mother that they didn't nominate him or lost his entry or something, but knowing his mother she would probably raise hell if he told her that.

So when the lunch bell rang he slowly made his way over to the main office where the poetry contest flyer was pinned on a bulletin board outside the office doors. He skimmed over the page that he had already read multiple times and brought his gaze to the bottom where it read:

TO ENTER, SUBMIT YOUR POEM TO EXTRACURRICULARS@RIDGEFIELDHIGH.COM.

Jamal knew exactly which poem he was going to submit, it was the one that he recited in his head every time he saw someone enjoying the company of their father—something that he had never experienced and probably never would.

He quickly typed out the email on his phone and went to press "send" but his finger hovered over the button like it had a mind of its own. He knew his mother was right and he wasn't worried about not being able to get 1st place, in fact, it was exactly the opposite. He was worried about drawing unwanted attention to himself if he did win. He felt isolated and misunderstood at Ridgefield High, and deep down he wanted to belong there but he wasn't sure this was going to help him with that secret dream. *What if it did though?* He found himself thinking. *How knows? Maybe I'll even find someone who loves poetry just as much as I do.*

With that hopeful thought spurring him on, he took the leap and sent the email; hoping that he hadn't just made his high school experience even harder than it already was.

As the day of the contest results grew closer, Jamal found himself feeling less and less nervous about it until he realized that he was actually a little bit excited. He just hoped against hope that whoever was going to decide the winner would take his poem into consideration because he had to admit that it would be really nice to win and have someone appreciate his talent.

When the day finally came, Jamal was a mixture of nervous nausea and excited jitters and he kept checking his phone every time a notification went off just in case it was the email declaring the winner.

By midday, Jamal decided that he needed to ignore his phone for a while and check back in later because constantly checking and feeling the bitter sting of disappointment when the email wasn't there was starting to get to him. He couldn't stay away from it for long, but his trick worked anyway because when he checked he saw an email notification from extracurriculars@ridgefieldhigh.com.

Nearly dropping his phone in excitement, Jamal rushed to type in his passcode and check the email, which read:

> Dear applicant,
>
> We are excited to consider your piece for 1st place in the Ridgefield High 3rd Annual Poetry Contest! All we need is your name and student ID so we can prepare for the announcement ceremony on Monday.
>
> Congratulations!

> Sincerely,
>
> Harry Norman, *Head of Ridgefield High Extra Curricular Program*

Jamal couldn't believe it. He quickly typed out a response with his name and student ID that thanked them profusely for considering his poem for 1st place and hit send before rushing downstairs to tell his mother the good news.

"I told you babycakes! They would have to be stupid to not recognize that talent you have honey," his mother said with a proud smile that warmed Jamal's heart. He felt like he was finally transcending the systemic barriers and racial prejudice that no one talked about at school; like he finally had a fighting chance to graduate and go to the University of California like he always wanted.

But that feeling evaporated as he looked down to check the ding from his phone that signaled Harry's response:

> Hello Jamal,
>
> Unfortunately, we have decided to go with another applicant.
>
> My apologies,
>
> Harry Norman, *Head of Ridgefield High Extra Curricular Program*

Jamal wanted to believe that it wasn't because of his name, because of his *race*, but the anger that spread across his mother's face when he told her convinced him otherwise.

She immediately grabbed her own phone to call the school and give them a piece of her mind, but Jamal convinced her not to. He didn't need any more unwanted attention from people who didn't understand him and would never treat him like they treated his fellow students with fairer skin.

She was so angry her knuckles were white from gripping her phone so tightly, but she must have seen the desperation in her son's eyes because she reluctantly put it down and wrapped him into a hug that was almost suffocating, like she was trying to squeeze the sadness right out of him.

The next day, the walk to school felt empty of the joy it usually held for him, and he stared at his feet as they shuffled along the pavement of the sidewalk. He wasn't sure why he looked up when he did—it wasn't like he didn't know where to go, he walked this route every day he went to school—but his gaze caught on a brightly colored flyer that was taped on the window of a shop ahead of him. This wasn't unusual, lots of shops put up flyers, but Jamal found himself drawn to this one for some reason. It wasn't until he walked closer to the shop window to read it that he realized why.

Alex

Some days Alex wished that she had never come out as bisexual. But most people assumed she was anyway, with her short-cropped brown hair and refusal to wear anything overly feminine. She just felt more comfortable in jeans and a T-shirt than a dress, and only wished that people would not judge her for what she wore or how she looked or who she was attracted to. That wasn't too much to ask, right? Apparently not—at least for the students at Ridgefield High.

She had never quite fit in with the other kids when she was growing up; she didn't like to play dolls or dress up like the girls her age did and the boys never treated her like an equal, so she often found herself playing alone or desperately trying (and failing) to fit in. The only thing that changed as she entered high school was that she had given up on trying to fit in. She openly embraced her sexuality and stopped trying to hide it since that never seemed to work anyway.

She had hoped that people would give up on judging her if she admitted that they were right to assume that she didn't like boys, but unfortunately it didn't work out that way. Instead, Alex found herself slinking down the hallways of Ridgefield High as she tried to be invisible so that Veronica Hilliard and her group of bird-brained lackeys wouldn't catch sight of her, but they always did. Apparently they really had nothing better to do than scan the hallways and pounce when they laid eyes on her, like they were the beady eyes of an eagle before it snatched up its prey.

Today was no different, except that Alex had stayed up way too late trying to study for her history exam after Veronica had snatched her notes out of her hands the day before and flushed them down the toilet, claiming that "freaks don't need to know history because they don't belong in it."

She had desperately hoped that they would leave her alone for at least the first half of the school day so she could focus on not failing her exam after they literally flushed her chances of passing down the toilet, but she should have known that they had no compassion when it came to her studies, or even her at all.

"What's the matter *freak*?" Veronica said as she and her goons surrounded Alex, blocking her from the door of her history class. "Have trouble sleeping?"

Alex scowled and stared down at her dusty men's sneakers, trying to hide the bags under her eyes that Veronica must have noticed.

"Come on Veronica, we're all gonna be late if you don't let me pass," Alex mumbled, not daring to challenge the bully by looking into her eyes.

"I don't need to be on time, Mr. Hubert actually likes me because I'm not a reject like you are," Veronica said venomously. Her flunkies giggled as if that was the funniest thing in the world.

Alex felt her cheeks burn as a mixture of shame and anger bubbled in her chest. She was so tired of this; so tired of being singled out just because she was different.

Suddenly, the school bell rang and Veronica smirked cruelly. "Saved by the bell I guess. Too bad there's nothing to save you from failing the history exam." She let out an airy fake laugh and turned on her heel. Her friends glared at Alex for a second longer, as if waiting to make sure her words really set in, before jutting their chins up in disgust and turning to follow Veronica into class.

Alex fumed there silently for a minute, making sure she was composed and as ready for her exam as she could be, before she slunk through the door behind them.

Alex wanted to get good grades, she really did. Her parents' didn't believe her though because her report cards never really showed much evidence of dedication or commitment to that goal. She knew she could do better if she had more support, but even the guidance counselor here judged her.

So she did her best on the history exam, but she struggled with most of the questions and knew her mark was going to reflect that. She felt herself becoming lightheaded as anxiety pumped itself into her bloodstream and she struggled to hold back the tears that threatened to stream down her pale skin. *It's not fair*, she thought to herself as she clenched her pencil in frustration. *I worked so hard on those notes.* She glanced up from her paper to catch a glimpse of Mr. Hubert, who was nose-deep in a book that looked older than he was—which was saying something because he looked at least 70. *Maybe if I just try to explain what happened then he might let me take it again.*

She took a deep breath and let that idea calm the volatile emotions that swirled inside her like a tornado of injustice and tried to focus on doing the best she could on the test. When it came time to hand in their papers, Alex hung back as unsuspiciously as she could as she waited for her classmates to leave the room.

"Mr. Hubert," she began as she walked up to his desk once the room was empty save the two of them, "I wanted to talk to you about something."

Mr. Hubert sighed dramatically and put down his book as he glanced up at her with a look that said *make it quick*.

Alex swallowed nervously, doing her best to quell the bile that tried to creep its way up her throat. "I, uh—well actually it wasn't me—but my notes got lost and I didn't have a chance to study for this test so I was wondering if you would let me take it again tomorrow?"

Mr. Hubert peered up at her from above the rim of his thin square glasses and smirked unpleasantly. "Let me guess—dog ate your homework?"

"No, that's not what happened at all. I worked hard on those notes and I didn't lose them—someone else did."

Mr. Hubert frowned in disappointment. "Miss Taylor, lying and blaming your mistakes on others is wildly immature and I will not tolerate such behavior."

"But I'm not lying! I swear it wasn't me," Alex said, wishing he would just believe her.

"Who did it then?"

Alex stared at her shoes for the second time this morning as she started to regret coming to Mr. Hubert at all. She should have known that he wouldn't support her.

"I'm waiting for an answer Miss Taylor," Mr. Hubert said impatiently.

"It was Veronica," Alex blurted out, unable to hold back anymore.

Mr. Hubert's face contorted with disgust and his eyes narrowed in anger. "How dare you accuse a girl like Veronica, *she* is an upstanding student who would never blame someone else for not doing their due diligence." He didn't say it, but the look on his face told her that he believed that was exactly what Alex had done to Veronica, not the other way around. Alex knew that nothing she said could convince him otherwise—she never should have tried to ask him for help. He would never see her as anything other than a freak, just like Veronica did.

Without another word, Alex slapped her paper on his desk and stormed out of his classroom. It was at that moment that she realized she couldn't stand the thought of being stuck in a school like this for another year. She was done with silently struggling and feeling unsupported, disrespected, and downright *hated* just because she was different.

As soon as she got home that night, she flicked open her laptop and began searching for another option that she could still enroll in for 12th Grade, since this school year was almost over already. There had to be some way for her to get the support and understanding she needed; the education she couldn't find at Ridgefield High. She had meant to just look for a different high school and convince her parents to let her transfer, but when she searched for "inclusive high school California" an article about a program called "Diversity Dawn Academy" grabbed her attention from the search results.

After doing a little research, she was set on Diversity Dawn Academy. It was still a part of Ridgefield High, but maybe it could provide the support and resources she needed to break free of the crippling chain of ignorance and bigotry that held her back at her current school.

When she finally closed her laptop and settled into bed just before midnight, Alex felt the tentative warmth of hope swell in her chest as she closed her eyes and envisioned the dawn of a bright new day lighting up her future.

Chapter 4:

The Threshold Crossed

Benjamin

Benjamin and Sarah smiled nervously at each other as they waited for everyone to arrive at the old community center for an introductory meeting with the students who had signed up for the program. Their parents and guardians were on the way as well, and Benjamin and Sarah knew how pivotal this initial prelude would be—they needed the first impressions to be good ones for the program to survive and thrive.

It seemed like a fitting place for the program to first spread its wings in an inaugural leap of faith, as the walls of the community center had hosted countless events and meetings across the years and was, in essence, the center of the community. The walls bore the faded remnants of past events, from washed-out posters of the bake sale fundraiser that took place when a storm had sent a tree crashing into the firehall to the more recent flyers for town meetings, chess tournaments, and talent shows. The building had facilitated the joining of community members in moments both mundane and monumental, and now it was ready to host the beginning of a fresh future with Diversity Dawn Academy as the vessel and Benjamin and Sarah at the helm.

The worn metal chairs were arranged in neat rows where they awaited the students and their parents much more patiently than the two educators at the front of the room did. They had set up a large easel in front of the chairs that was equipped with lesson plans, schedules, and lined paper in case they needed to write something out during the meeting. Two chairs sat beside it so they could address the room from a comforting position as opposed to looming over them. They had also placed a table against the wall beside the door so that the students and their parents could enjoy a fresh pot of coffee and an assortment of baked goods from the bakery down the street.

They had thought of everything, which is why they were so anxious for the program's future members to arrive and the meeting to commence, because waiting without anything to do but wonder what might go wrong was torture.

It didn't take long for people to begin tentatively streaming in as the clock above the door clicked closer to 9:00 a.m. Benjamin and Sarah were shocked by the number of people who arrived, but they could tell that they were just as nervous—if not more—than the educators themselves were. Weariness and caution painted the faces of the people who entered the building, and Benjamin knew he had to do everything he could to convince them that they made the right choice by coming here.

He nodded in acknowledgment to some of his students who had made the choice to join the program and smiled warmly at everyone, with Sarah doing the same beside him.

"Welcome to Diversity Dawn Academy," Benjamin said after they had all settled into their seats. "We're not just a school—we're a journey. A place where curiosity is our compass, where learning transcends textbooks. We'll stumble, we'll fall, but we'll rise together." As confident as he felt when he said those words, the crowd seated in front of him didn't seem too convinced.

"I know how daunting this may seem, and I know you're all wondering why we should leave the familiar for the unknown; why you should place your, or your children's, future on an untested venture. These feelings are caused by the vertigo that travels up your spine as you stand on the precipice of a new horizon; an education that won't let you down or leave you feeling unsupported or lost. You all came here for a reason, whether you know it or not. You're here because you're hungry for change, because you know that the traditional education system can't—and hasn't—supported you in the ways that you need, the ways you deserve. Let this program be a stepping stone for a future that is yours to claim; a new dawn that shines an all-encompassing light of hope on your chances of success," Benjamin said, and every word that left his lips tingled with truth and power.

Expressions shifted slowly from the furrowed eyebrows of unease and caution to eyes bright with curiosity and lips spread in tentative smiles. Sarah smiled proudly at Benjamin and together they dove into the rest of the meeting, covering lesson plans and schedules and showcasing the stories of successful alternative education programs that had jaw-dropping graduation rates. They screened questions afterward, reassuring the positive aspects of the programs and squashing the misinformed rumors that had spread from the seeds of doubt and apprehension. The overall effect of the presentation turned the tides of the uncertainty that had filled people's hearts when they first walked into the building.

When they were finished, the nervous tension in the air had decreased significantly and Benjamin could tell that everyone, including himself, was feeling less unsure of the program's outcomes.

"Please feel free to enjoy the delicious pastries from Betty's Bakery and the fresh coffee on the table there while we take a moment to mingle and all get familiar with each other," Sarah said warmly. Benjamin and Sarah went around the room as people milled about and introduced themselves.

A young girl with thick, dark hair and tan skin introduced herself as Maria. She was reserved and cautious, but Benjamin could see the fire that shone brightly in her eyes and knew that she was holding back her true self. He made a mental note to help draw her out of her shell before she graduated so she could embrace her true personality as she stepped into the world of adulthood. Her parents seemed nervous as well, and Benjamin did his best to try and make them feel as welcome as possible as he introduced himself. Their answers were brief and he got the feeling that they didn't want to talk, so he didn't press and instead thanked them for coming before he left to meet other students and families. He mentally promised himself that he would do his best to make them gradually feel more comfortable here because he wanted everyone to feel welcome.

He then saw one of his previous students, Kaylee Hudson, blushing as she talked with a young African-American boy who smiled shyly at her. "I'm so glad you came Kaylee, this program is going to be perfect for you," Benjamin said as he walked up to them. Kaylee suffered from social anxiety and struggled to find support at Ridgefield High. She was one of the students that Benjamin fought so hard to provide for with this program.

"Mr. Diamonds, hi, thank you. I'm excited." Benjamin could tell she was feeling a bit flustered around the boy she was obviously attracted to. "Hello young man, thank you for taking the leap to apply for Diversity Dawn Academy," Benjamin said as he smiled warmly at the boy. "I'm Mr. Diamonds, Kaylee's old—and new—math teacher. What's your name?"

"Hello Mr. Diamond, I'm Jamal Robinson. It's nice to meet you too," Jamal said as Benjamin shook his hand.

"Well I'll leave you two to it, have fun and don't forget to do your math homework before class starts!" Benjamin chuckled as their eyes went wide in surprise. "I'm just kidding, class has got to start before I give out homework. Take care you two, see you Monday!"

He shook his head and chuckled again at his own joke as he walked away from them and towards a young girl with extremely short brown hair and pale skin. She stood beside her parents awkwardly, and Benjamin could tell that they weren't as close as some families were. He could also see from her body language that the young girl was nervous and her eyes darted around the room anxiously. He put on his most comforting smile and walked up to her slowly but purposefully.

"Hello, my name is Benjamin Diamonds, I'm the co-founder of Diversity Dawn Academy and I'll be your math teacher. What's your name?"

"Alex," she said. She seemed cautious and cold, and Benjamin wondered what kind of experience she must have had with a teacher to make her so jaded against him. He promised himself that he would prove to her that he was there to support and uplift her, not drag her down like people had obviously done in the past.

"It's nice to meet you Alex, and these are your parents?" he asked, directly his gaze at the adults beside her and smiling. She nodded silently. He reached out and shook each of their hands. They too, seemed cold and distant, and Benjamin hoped he would be able to change that by the end of the school year. "Thank you all for coming. I'm excited to start this journey together; I promise you it will be worth it."

"Thank you. We're going to head out now, I have a plane to catch," Alex's father said curtly. He had the air of a businessman about him, and he didn't seem very invested in the meeting. Benjamin did his best to hide his disdain and instead smiled at him again.

"Well it was nice to meet you all. Safe travels Mr.?" Benjamin said.

"Taylor."

"Thanks again for coming Mr. and Mrs. Taylor. I look forward to seeing you in class on Monday Alex," Benjamin said with a smile.

They left without another word, and Benjamin found himself looking forward to the challenge of breaking their stigmas and getting to know Alex. She seemed like a strong-willed young woman with a bright future ahead of her. He made his way across the room and found Sarah, who seemed to have finished her introductions as well.

They smiled and stood by the door as they bid everyone goodbye and thanked them for coming before closing the door and turning to look at each other. They shared a warm look that said everything without even needing to say a word—they had just crossed a threshold for Diversity Dawn Academy, and their eyes were filled with the sparkle of hope as they realized how ready they were for what was to come.

Chapter 5:

The First Lesson

Benjamin

Benjamin and Sarah had spent so long preparing for this day, so many hours planning and double-checking and visualizing, that it felt surreal now that the time had come to welcome their first students to the program's initial class.

Everything was ready—the portable classrooms had just recently finished being constructed and furnished with second-hand desks and chairs because the budget was so tight, and the lesson plans were prepped and ready to go—but Benjamin still felt the powerful tremors of anxiety rock him to his core. He had put everything into this program, and the dark feeling of doubt snuck its way into his mind like a serpent slithering its way into a crevice. *What if it doesn't work out and I can't help my students because all this was for nothing?* He clutched a nearby desk to steady himself as his own mind turned against him in a flurry of panic.

As always, Sarah read him like a book and was there to calm his thoughts and bring him back to reality. "Hey," she said, approaching him with a comforting smile, "it's going to go just fine. We've triple-checked everything—we're ready and you know it, so just take a deep breath and remember that we got this."

Benjamin took a deep, shaky breath in and smiled at Sarah as the familiar warmth of gratitude for her presence swelled in his chest.

"You always know what to say," he said with a chuckle, feeling the heavy weight of anxiety lift off his chest as her words settled in.

"It's not that hard, I just know what you need to hear because I understand you," Sarah said, and Benjamin found himself lost in her deep hazel eyes as he realized just how much she really did understand him. But he didn't have a chance to consider what that meant to him before the door opened and their first student stepped in.

"Good morning Kaylee! It's nice to see a familiar face here bright and early," Benjamin said as he tore himself from his thoughts and turned to face the young girl.

"Good morning Mr. Diamonds and Ms. Mitchell," Kaylee said with a timid smile. She had always been a bit shy, and it had taken Benjamin a lot of effort to make her feel comfortable and less nervous in his presence as she seemed to fear authority figures. Benjamin wasn't sure what kind of trauma that stemmed from, but he was determined to help her move through it so that it didn't affect her grades and thereby her future.

It didn't take long before the rest of the students arrived, some of which were new to him and some that he had taught in his class at Ridgefield High, and all of them were on time. All of them, that is, except a young boy that Benjamin had met at the meeting on Friday night. His name was Brody Walsh and he had walked in 15 minutes past 9:00 a.m. when class was supposed to start. Normally, Benjamin offered his students a chance to explain themselves because there's always a reason behind being late. He was especially lenient on the first day of class because everyone was adjusting to where they had to go and getting used to their new schedules, but he always asked for an explanation because it usually helped him realize what the source of their tardiness was. And by knowing the source, Benjamin could then help the student themselves understand and overcome it. However, it seemed like Brody was late on purpose because he just didn't want to be there, and that was the hardest source of tardiness to cure.

Showing up late and making a scene of how uninterested he was seemed like a cry for attention to Benjamin, and he wondered if the young boy was getting enough attention from his parents or if he was currently experiencing instability at home. One of the reasons he pondered this was because it had only been his mother who showed up with him at the meeting—and it was obvious from both of their demeanors that he had no interest in the program. It appeared that his mother had signed him up in a desperate attempt to get him on the right track because, according to the school records that Benjamin had looked into, his grades were suffering from his rebellious attitude. Benjamin suspected that what he needed was the support and resources that Diversity Dawn Academy could offer, so he looked forward to helping him turn his future around. He made a mental note to ask him to stay for a minute after class so he could constructively discuss his tardiness without having the rest of the students as an audience.

"Good morning everyone, and welcome to the first day of Ridgefield High's new alternative education program. We are very excited to get to know you all a bit better, whether we know you from previous classes or not, and to have you all here as pioneers of the education model that will shape our future," Benjamin addressed the class after they had all settled into their desks.

"This is your homeroom, where Ms. Mitchell here is going to teach you all English," Benjamin said as he gestured to Sarah beside him. She smiled warmly at the class. "I will see you afterwards in the portable classroom beside us for math class. I leave you in her capable hands until then."

Sarah

Sarah smiled at the students who sat before her, feeling excited and honored to be the first class that they got to experience in the program.

"I want you all to know that this is a safe space and that you can trust me, but I know that might be hard for some of you to feel comfortable with since trust is earned and some people may have broken your trust in the past. So I've prepared a bit of an ice-breaker activity that might help you all get to know each other a bit more and understand the path that led you to this classroom. I'm going to participate as well so that you can get to know me too and hopefully familiarity can eventually lead to trust," Sarah said, sitting on the edge of her own desk at the front of the room so she could address the class from a casual position and hopefully put them at ease.

She wanted them to know that this class was not like other English classes, and that she was not like other English teachers. She was here to support and uplift them, and to do that she wanted to seem as approachable as possible.

"I want you all to take a moment to think about what has brought you here, about why you feel a new dawn could change your life and why alternative education appealed to you. If you didn't bring a notebook or paper, I have some here that you can write out your thoughts on," Sarah said, tapping a pile of paper on the desk beside her. "I also have pencils, notebooks, and duotangs if you need those as well." She had purchased all of it with her own money since the program's budget was so tight, but they didn't need to worry about that.

"When you've written at least a small paragraph that encompasses all the feelings you have surrounding this class—your expectations, your fears, your hopes for the future—then I encourage you to share it with the class." Sarah watched as many of the students squirmed in their seats, obviously uncomfortable at the thought of sharing such intimate feelings with people they hardly knew.

"If you don't want to speak out loud you don't have to, you can have your paper passed around or not share at all—that's completely fine, I just want you all to sit with those emotions after you've written them out."

Sarah had already prepared her own paragraph for the activity, it was sitting on a piece of paper right beside her on the desk, but she didn't really need it—she could simply speak from the heart about why she was there.

A few students came up to her desk to grab some supplies and soon the only sound that filled the room was the scratching of pencils against paper as they wrote out their answers to the activity. She looked out the window of the classroom as she waited and enjoyed the bright colors of the fall season until the sound dissipated and she turned to see that no one was writing anymore.

"Is everyone finished?" she asked. "If not, take your time. I'm sure some of the reasons you're here might be hard to grapple with, so I can understand how challenging it may feel to express them on paper."

No one had an answer to that, and no one seemed to be writing still, so Sarah assumed that they were all done.

"Does anyone want to share what they wrote?"

An uncomfortable silence filled the room as the students fidgeted in a unanimous "no."

"That's okay, I understand. I'll go first and maybe someone will feel like sharing after," Sarah said with a comforting smile, trying to ease the tension from the room.

"When I was young, I always knew I wanted to be a teacher. From the moment I knew what teaching was, it called to me like a siren's song. I was bullied a lot as a child because I was heavier than most, and so my school was not a safe place for me. I never got the support I needed and no one seemed to care or even believe that I was suffering from the negative effects that bullying can inflict on a young child. I experienced first-hand how mangled and tired the education system was as I struggled to move through it, and I knew that something had to change. I had hoped that by the time I obtained my teaching degree that would have happened already, but unfortunately not much has been updated since I noticed the failings of the traditional school system at a young age. I'm here today because I don't want any of you to have to suffer like I did; I want you to know that I'm here for you and I will believe you if you come to me seeking support," Sarah said, looking at the students who sat before her.

She made eye contact with Alex, the young girl she had met at the meet and greet on Friday, and saw understanding shine in her wide green eyes from where she sat at the back of the class. Sarah suspected that she might have suffered from a similar experience with bullying, and she felt compassion and respect bloom inside her as she observed the strength in the young girl's eyes. Sarah knew how unbearable bullying can be and how much of a negative impact it can have on grades, so she was proud that Alex had taken the leap to try alternative education and foster the resilience that obviously was already present in her. She wanted to hear her story and bond with her over their shared experiences, but she had a feeling that might be hard for her.

"Did anyone change their mind and want to share now?" Sarah asked, tentatively prodding her students to emerge from their shells. She glanced at Alex again, hoping to encourage her to share by expressing her genuine intrigue through eye contact, but Alex frowned slightly and looked down at her desk. She clearly wasn't ready to share, and Sarah wasn't going to push her.

"That's okay, we'll get there. You don't even have to hand in those papers to me if you don't feel comfortable with that, I just wanted to help you all realize why you're here and visualize what you want from this program."

Sarah glanced down at the dainty gold watch that was wrapped around her wrist. Benjamin had bought it for her when they were still in the process of preparing Diversity Dawn Academy for its first semester because he claimed she was never on time. She had laughed because she was only ever a few minutes late at most, but the ex-marine in him must've wanted her to grow out of it. It was a lovely watch though, and Sarah thought of him whenever she looked at it. This time her thoughts were especially on him, because it was almost time for his class to start. She thought about how nervous he was this morning and hoped that he would be okay. She wasn't too worried though, she knew he was a great teacher who cared about his students more than anything.

She tore herself from her thoughts as she realized she must have been looking at the watch for too long. "Well, that just about wraps up our first class," she said with a smile. "You can leave those papers with me if you want to, or not, and then head over to the other portable for math class with Mr. Diamonds."

She hopped off the edge of her desk as the students got up to leave and instantly regretted sitting there for so long—all the blood had sank to her legs and made them feel like lead as she tried to walk—so she sank into the soft leather chair that sat behind her desk. After their collective reluctance to share, Sarah was not expecting anyone to leave her with their paragraph, but she made herself get up once her legs felt normal again to check if there were any left on the desks.

Unsurprisingly, she passed empty desk after empty desk and was just about ready to assume that none of them had wanted to see their paragraphs when suddenly she caught sight of one on the desks at the back of the class. She knew instantly who it belonged to.

Chapter 6:

In the Moonlight

Benjamin

Benjamin was alone in the staff room, needing a chance to sit down after the day that he had. His first class had been even better than he had anticipated it would be, but he couldn't deny that it left him feeling drained. He had been so anxious about making sure that everything went perfectly that he had nearly lost sight of what he really needed to do at that moment—be a calm, collected role model for his students to look up to, especially on the first day of an untested program. They were probably even more nervous than he was.

His chest filled with warmth as he realized how grateful he was that Sarah had been there to calm him down, just like she always was. But then his brows furrowed as he realized that he didn't know what he would do without her, and that he found himself growing attached to her in a way that he had never felt with any other colleague. He quickly shoved the thought aside, knowing that she had only recently ended things with her boyfriend that she had been seeing for six years. Benjamin knew she was still getting over him and didn't want to get in the way of that process or make anything complicated.

Benjamin knew this because Sarah broke down one night when they had stayed up too late working on the final touches of the program. He suspected that the stress had crumpled her to a point where she couldn't keep her feelings at bay anymore because she started talking about her failed love life after a long silence that had sat heavily between them. She told him through her sobs that her ex had just proposed to her at the time and everything had been perfect, until she found out that he had been cheating on her for years. It only came to light when they announced their engagement, because the woman he was having an affair with had been oblivious to Sarah's existence in the man's life until she heard the news. She immediately told Sarah what had been happening, so Sarah admitted that she wasn't even mad at the woman because she had been tricked just like she had.

He could only imagine how heart-wrenching that must be for her to process, so he promised himself that he would give her the space she needed and not even consider thinking about her in any way that wasn't entirely professional or platonic, because she didn't need any more confusion in her love life right now. *Besides, maybe I'm just overtired and my brain is playing tricks on me. After all, I've never thought about Sarah like this before.* Benjamin thought to himself. *Or have I?* He thought back to all the times he'd felt the warm glow of gratitude swell in his chest from her presence and wondered if it had been a subtle sign of even deeper feelings that he had simply been too worried about getting the program ready to acknowledge.

As if summoned by his thoughts, he was torn from contemplating his feelings by the telltale confident footsteps that announced Sarah's entrance into the staff room. He glanced up from the papers that were strewn across the table and smiled at her as she approached him. Her deep hazel eyes were as bright and determined as they always were, but her shoulders looked like they were suffering to bear the weight of exhaustion. She smiled back at him, and if he couldn't tell before, he would've known she was tired from the feeble smile that she gave him.

"How did your class go?" he asked as she plopped down in the chair beside him.

"Not as well as I was hoping to be honest, but I should've known that they weren't going to be ready to share such intimate sides of themselves on the first day. I'll try a lighter team-building exercise tomorrow," Sarah said with a sigh. "I think I got through to one of the students though—Alex left her paper for me to read."

"None of the other students did?"

Sarah shook her head sadly. "No, but it was a lot to ask since I'm practically a total stranger at this point."

"Don't worry, you'll gain their trust soon," Benjamin reassured her, wanting to be the one to offer support for once.

"Thanks Ben," she said as she smiled warmly at him. She was the only one who could call him by his nickname—he would correct anyone else who tried—but he liked the way it sounded coming from her lips.

"How did your class go?" she asked.

"It went well actually. Everyone built structurally sound towers and I think they bonded a bit in the process. I didn't pick a winner, there was no need for that, but I think they all did well even without the incentive," Benjamin said proudly.

"That's good, even Brody got involved?" Sarah asked hesitantly. She must've also noticed that he seemed to be a harder case to crack than most.

"To a certain extent," Benjamin replied. "He didn't seem very committed at first, but he got into it after awhile and I think he might have even bonded a bit with Jamal."

"That's great, I think he could use a friend and Jamal seems like he could be a good influence on him," Sarah said.

Benjamin nodded. "Yeah that's what I was thinking too."

Suddenly the weight of his exhaustion hit him as he let his body release all the tension it had been holding from the stress of wanting the first day to go well. Talking with Sarah helped him let go of a symbolic breath he hadn't realized he'd been holding all day. It was like he could finally unwind now that she was here beside him.

He looked at her and smiled, and she smiled back, lighting her face up in a way that made her even more beautiful. *Why did I never notice how beautiful she is?* Benjamin wondered to himself.

They sat in comfortable silence for a moment, and Benjamin found himself longing to spend more time with her instead of leaving the staff room alone.

"Hey, have you had dinner yet? I was thinking of heading over to that Italian restaurant down the street, would you like to join me? My treat—we deserve to celebrate after all the work we put into making today go smoothly." Benjamin was surprised by the words that left his lips, he had not intended to ask her out to dinner when he opened his mouth to speak, but it came out unbidden as if his lips had a mind of their own.

A slow smile spread across Sarah's face, and Benjamin wondered if she was just as surprised as he was by his invitation to dinner.

"You mean Giorgio's? That place is pretty expensive, are you sure?" she asked.

"Yeah, like I said we deserve to treat ourselves after working so hard to bring the program to life these last couple months, and it's my way of thanking you for making this all possible," Benjamin said with a warm smile. He didn't know what had come over him, but he found himself more forward than he usually was. Usually it was Sarah who was the forward one.

Sarah smiled again, even brighter than before, and Benjamin found himself in awe of the warmth that radiated off her. "Okay then, your car or mine?"

"I can drive and drop you off tonight and then we can carpool to work tomorrow," Benjamin offered.

Sarah smiled as her cheeks reddened ever so slightly and Benjamin wondered if she too just realized how much this was starting to sound like a date. He hoped it wasn't making her feel weird about the whole thing, because the last thing he wanted was to make her uncomfortable.

She didn't seem very unsettled on the drive to the restaurant though, so Benjamin told himself that it was only him who was making their dinner seem more intimate than it was. After all, they were just colleagues getting a bite to eat and celebrating a big win, right?

Except Benjamin found it harder to believe that sentence as they struggled to tear their eyes off each other during their dinner. Sarah's laughter twinkled in the air as they talked about anything but work and simply enjoyed each other's company, and Benjamin couldn't remember the last time he had this much fun on any date he'd ever been on. But he had to keep reminding himself that it wasn't a date and that they were just close friends who had been through a lot together.

By the time they had finished eating and headed out to Benjamin's car, the sun had already dipped below the horizon and the full moon had risen up to set the streets awash in its pale blue glow as Benjamin drove Sarah home. Sarah turned on the radio and rolled up the volume knob as *Dreams* by Fleetwood Mac tumbled out of Benjamin's car speakers.

"I love this song," she said over the lyrics as she started swaying to the rhythm.

Benjamin had admittedly never paid much attention to the song, but as he watched Sarah close her eyes and softly sing the lyrics he decided that it was now one of his favorites. It would always remind him of this moment, and he never wanted to forget the way Sarah looked in the moonlight tonight.

The drive to Sarah's house wasn't long enough, because Benjamin wasn't ready for this night to end, but soon enough he was parked in her driveway. Without thinking, he hopped out of the car and walked over to open her door for her before he realized how weird that might be since this wasn't a date. *I can still be respectful without it being romantic*, he told himself.

Sarah chuckled as she stepped out of the car. "Thanks Ben, for everything. I really needed this," she said as she gazed up at him.

Benjamin wanted to say something, something smooth or funny or even just coherent, but his words failed him as he found himself mesmerized by the way her eyes twinkled in the moonlight.

She chuckled warmly again, and he coughed to regain his composure.

"No problem Sarah, you deserve it. I meant it when I said it was my way of thanking you for all that you've done for me. You walked into my life and changed it for the better, so the least I could do was pay for a nice dinner," Benjamin said with a sheepish smile.

"You've changed my life too, and I'm so glad I met you," Sarah said. She reached up on her tiptoes to brush a kiss against his cheek, sending an electric shock shooting up his spine. "Goodnight Ben, see you tomorrow."

Benjamin was speechless as she pulled away from him and smiled before walking up to her front porch. She turned as she opened her door and waved at him. He waved feebly back, feeling too shell-shocked to manage anything more. He was sure that a dumbstruck grin was plastered across his face though, because his cheeks were starting to hurt from smiling so wide. He climbed into his car and drove home in the moonlight, feeling lighter than air and wondering if maybe it was a date after all.

Chapter 7:

Broken Trust

Benjamin

Benjamin woke up feeling like nothing could bring him down from the high that he was riding after his night with Sarah. He was smiling so much that by the time he had gotten ready to leave his house for work his cheeks were hurting from the grin that was stretched across his face.

He picked up Sarah so they could carpool to work together, and the smile she gave him when he pulled into her driveway made his heart sing. They listened to the radio and didn't say much during the short drive to the school, but the air between them buzzed with an electricity that neither of them addressed.

He walked into the school feeling like he had his very own ray of sunshine that beamed down on him and brightened his day, until a storm cloud known as Mr. Peters blew in and stole his sunshine away.

"What do you mean you're cutting our budget?" Benjamin asked incredulously as he sat in front of the school board once again. He and Sarah had been called to a sudden meeting this morning, and the flame of pure ecstasy that Benjamin's heart had been fueled with mere moments ago was drowned by the leaden feeling of dread as they heard the news.

"Unfortunately," Evan said in a way that sounded like he didn't think it was unfortunate at all, "other matters have arisen that take precedence, so we are reducing your budget by 25% to accommodate the adjustment."

Benjamin and Sarah sat aghast in their seats for a moment as they tried to process this unexpected turn of events.

"Twenty-five percent? We already have to pay for extraneous expenditures like notebooks and pencils from our own pockets, how on earth do you expect us to pay the staff with 25% of our budget missing?" Sarah said, her tone low and clipped and her face red as she struggled to keep her composure. It seemed to be an occurring theme: Sitting in front of the board wore her patience so thin she had to avoid lashing out at the ignorance that threatened to snuff out the program they had worked so hard to bring to life.

Benjamin was just as upset as she was, but he internalized his turmoil of emotions and kept them locked inside of him like a swirling tornado of turbulent chords. He couldn't afford to lose his temper, and his time as a Marine taught him how to keep his emotions in check. That didn't mean he wasn't fuming on the inside though.

"I'd like to know what is so important that it takes priority over the well-being of the marginalized students who rely on the only alternative education system in this part of the city?" Benjamin asked through gritted teeth.

"If you must know, we're investing in upgrading our social media platforms. We need to be able to reach more members of our community and potentially increase graduation rates," George Harrington huffed indignantly.

"But alternative education models have consistently proven their ability to dramatically increase graduation rates. There's evidence everywhere, just take a look at the data!" Sarah said, slamming her hands on the table in front of her and leaning forward in her seat.

"We have no experience with such findings, and I suggest that you control yourself Ms. Mitchell or you shall be your program's undoing," Miriam Jenkins spat, her eyes narrowed with disapproval.

Benjamin threw a pleading glance at both Peter Howes and Quinn Jackson, but Quinn stared down at the table and avoided eye contact and Peter imperceptibly shook his head sadly with a helpless look that told him there was nothing the board member could do.

Sarah was fuming silently beside him, and Benjamin knew that if they stayed in this room any longer the chance of her temper flying loose would increase drastically every time Evan opened his mouth to say something. So he sighed and stood up from his chair, motioning for Sarah to do the same. Benjamin knew he should say something to clear the air but he didn't trust himself to lest he say something that might only make matters worse. He himself was struggling to rein in his temper as he felt the program's chances of being approved after the two-year pilot slip through his fingers.

He and Sarah marched silently to the staff room, but other teachers filled the crowded space so they made their way to Benjamin's car in the parking lot.

When they arrived, Benjamin couldn't help but remember how happy he was this morning when he and Sarah had been in his car last, and how much had changed in such a short time. Benjamin felt his heart harden as he realized that whatever was going on between them was going to have to wait because the program was in jeopardy and it came before everything else.

They sat in his car and furtively attempted to brainstorm solutions for the budget cut, but by the time they had to get ready for classes to start they had run out of feasible ideas. With a heavy heart, Benjamin wished Sarah good luck with her class as she walked into the first portable classroom and he retreated to the portable next to it where he taught his class. He sat at his desk and quickly flicked open his laptop as he remembered that Diversity Dawn Academy had donors who had contributed to the program when it was first introduced and in need of financial support to get started—because the budget was tight enough to begin with even before it got cut.

Benjamin silently cursed the school board for putting him in this position as he realized who the program's biggest donor was. He spent the rest of his time before his class started trying to figure out a different solution, but by the time his students started streaming through the door he realized that there was no other option.

***

Benjamin's heart had never felt as heavy in his chest as it did when he looked up at the huge, sleek modern house that was sprawled out on top of a hill in front of him. He knew he shouldn't have even considered coming here, but he had no choice. He told himself that Sarah would understand if she ever found out, but deep down he knew otherwise.

He walked up to the flawless white door and rang the doorbell, wishing someone else would come to open it. But apparently not all wishes come true, because Oliver Benedict—the man who had crushed Sarah's heart like a worthless grape that meant nothing to him—opened the door and flashed him a brilliant white smile. He was tall and fit, with tan skin and dark hair that was short on the sides and immaculately styled at the top of his head. He smelled of expensive cologne and his clothes were spotless and crisp. In other words, he looked just as rich as was.

"Benjamin, hello!" he said, like they had known each other for years and Benjamin hadn't only ever talked to him on the phone the day before to arrange this meeting. "Please, come in."

Benjamin followed the millionaire into his home and down a long hallway into his office, where he was offered a drink after he sat down in a luscious white leather chair.

"Are you sure?" Oliver asked when Benjamin politely declined the glass that was extended to him. "This is twelve year old whiskey."

"I don't drink, thank you though."

Oliver shrugged and brought his own glass to the chair behind a huge desk in front of Benjamin that was carved from a large slab of mahogany.

"So, you came here to talk about Diversity Dawn Academy," Oliver said as he sipped his drink.

"Yes, our budget has been cut and we can't afford to pay our staff. Without a significant donation, the program will flounder and we'll be forced to shut it down before it even has a real chance to get running," Benjamin said, wishing he didn't have to be here. He had never been one to ask for favors, and this was the last person he wanted to ask anything of—ever. Yet here he was, betraying Sarah's trust and probably throwing away whatever had blossomed between them that night under the moon, because he knew the program had no other chance of survival.

Oliver sipped his drink again and stared at the ice cubes as he seemed to consider Benjamin's plea for help.

"And this will make Sarah happy?" he asked quietly, showing a vulnerability that Benjamin wasn't expecting. *Why should he care? He's the one who didn't care enough to not break her heart.*

Benjamin faltered for a moment before he could respond. "I can't speak for Sarah, but I know she was devastated by the budget cut." It was all he could bring himself to say, and he wondered if he should have said it at all.

Oliver sat up in his seat and beamed. "That's all I had to hear—if it'll make her happy then I'm in."

Benjamin still couldn't convince his brain to believe the words his ears were receiving, but he wasn't about to turn down the money that Diversity Dawn Academy so desperately needed. So he stood up as Oliver did and shook the man's hand—the man who had cheated on Sarah and broke her trust. And as he did, he realized that while he hadn't cheated on Sarah (they weren't even in a position where that was possible) he had broken her trust, so he wasn't much better than the man she had spent the last couple of months crying over.

Sarah

Benjamin was acting weird. It had started when he suddenly told her that the budget issue was fixed by some mysterious donor, and when she asked who it was he dodged her question. She knew something was up, and she was not going to tolerate being unaware of major decisions that affected the future of Diversity Dawn Academy. She had put too much into the program to be shut out like that, and it hurt that Benjamin would be the one to do it to her. She had just started to feel closer to him than anyone else she had met after Oliver broke her trust, and she wasn't going to let this budget cut fiasco come between them.

So she dove into the program's financial records and dug up the transaction history so she could find out who had donated money to save Diversity Dawn Academy. It didn't take her long to find it, but when she did her heart plummeted and she wished she hadn't even bothered to look.

The sight of her ex-fiancé's name sent her into shock, and she had to force herself to breathe after a breathless moment as she realized why Benjamin had tried to hide this from her. She reeled with betrayal as tears clouded her vision, and she slammed her laptop closed so she didn't have to stare at Oliver's name anymore.

She bolted out of her seat and stormed out of her apartment, grabbing her keys and throwing on her shoes before stomping to her car and slamming the door shut as she turned the ignition.

It was raining by the time she had arrived at Benjamin's apartment, but she was too angry to care. She stepped out in the drenching downpour and slammed her fist against Benjamin's door. He opened it in a heartbeat, like he had been waiting for her to arrive.

"Sarah, what are doing? It's freezing out here, come inside," he said, motioning for her to come in so he could close the door.

"Why did you do it?" she said, ignoring the rain and everything else that wasn't the look of dread that crept onto Benjamin's face.

"Sarah I'm so sorry, there was no other way—" he began, but Sarah cut him off before he could finish.

"Of course there was another way! We could've figured it out together, but you went behind my back and asked *him* for money! How could you? You know what he did to me," Sarah said as her tears started flowing freely and intermingling with the rain that streamed down her face.

"Sarah I—"

"No, you know what? No. I trusted you, I even started to—" She shook her head, not letting herself finish that sentence.

Benjamin hung his head in silence, refusing to look her in the eyes.

"I can't believe you," she said as she closed her eyes in frustration and sorrow. "I have to go."

"Sarah, wait," he called out after her as she turned to leave, but she didn't even bother turning back to look at him before she got back into her car and peeled out of his driveway. By the time she made it back to her apartment, she was completely drenched and the cold had seeped its way into her bones. She stripped the wet clothes off her body and stepped into the shower in an effort to warm herself up, but no matter how hot her body got she still felt numb with pain. She thought she had dried up all the tears she had after crying about Oliver for so long, but her tears never stopped flowing until her head hit her pillow and exhaustion took over.

***

Sarah did her best to avoid Benjamin as much as possible in the days that followed, but it was hard when she worked so closely with him. The air between them was fraught with tension and anguish, and Sarah's heart had hardened with the anger that flared within her every time she saw his face.

She knew this couldn't go on for much longer, but she wasn't sure what to do. She wasn't ready to forgive him for what he did and she didn't know if she ever would be, but she couldn't just leave Diversity Dawn Academy after all that she had put into it. It was her life's purpose culminated into a single program, and she refused to walk away from it because a man had broken her heart again.

Which is why, when he approached her one day when they were alone in the staff room after all the students had gone home, she didn't immediately turn and walk away like she had every other time he tried to talk to her. She hadn't been ready to hear his side of the story yet, but she was too tired to fight anymore.

"Sarah I'm so sorry," Benjamin said, and his eyes were so full of sorrow and remorse that Sarah had to look down to stop the tears that threatened to well up in her own eyes.

She said nothing and just continued to stare down at the cheap linoleum flooring, but she didn't leave so Benjamin seemed to take it as a sign to continue speaking.

"I never should have gone behind your back, we've been in this together from the very beginning and it was wrong of me to make that decision without you to begin with, especially considering who I made it with instead," Benjamin said. Sarah could hear the earnest in his voice but she still refused to look him in the eyes.

"I broke your trust and you had just started to feel comfortable with trusting someone again. It was the worst thing I've ever done in my life and I can't sleep at night knowing that I did that to you." Sarah believed that he hadn't been sleeping, she had noticed the bags under his eyes starting to form.

"I just want to make it right," Benjamin continued. "I miss you—you're the best part of my day and I can't make it through this without you. I need you, this program needs you, and I want to make it up to you."

Sarah tore her gaze from the floor and looked up into his eyes for any hint of dishonesty in them. All she found was raw, unfiltered emotions that shone in the reflection of his irises—from pain to sorrow to remorse—and she knew that he was telling her the truth.

He must have read the shift in her demeanor because he launched into a babble of words, as if he thought she might change her mind if he didn't speak fast enough.

"Please let me try and make it right, just meet me at the park tomorrow at 3 and I promise I'll do everything in my power to fix this."

Sarah wasn't sure anything could fix the jumbled mess that stood between them and kept them apart, but she missed the way they used to be—and she knew she couldn't stay mad at him forever because she had to work with him—so she was willing to give it a try. Without saying a word or breaking eye contact, she nodded slowly and watched as Benjamin's shoulders slumped in relief.

"Thank you, this means everything," he said as he gathered his things and prepared to leave. "I have to go get ready. I'll see you tomorrow, okay?"

Sarah nodded silently again, not trusting herself to speak, and watched as he quickly made his way out the door. With a sigh, she began gathering her own things and wondering what on earth he had planned for tomorrow.

Benjamin

Benjamin knew exactly what he had to do to make things right. It was risky—it could potentially go sideways and make everything worse instead of mending broken bonds—but this time he really didn't have any other choice. He had to fix things with him and Sarah. The last few days had been torture for him; guilt and regret had been eating him alive like the caustic burn of a poison that could only be cured by mending the rift that he had put between him and Sarah. So he found himself back at the place where the whole fiasco started, but this time he was determined to right the wrong he had done.

This time, when he saw Oliver's face, he wasn't unsure of himself or wracked with guilt. This time he had a plan.

"I need to talk to you," Benjamin said at the sight of Oliver's surprised face. The confusion set in the lines on the rich man's forehead creased even further at Benjamin's demand, but he let him in without a fuss, clearly curious to find out what Benjamin was so dead set on talking with him about.

And so Benjamin once again entered the house of the man who had broken Sarah's heart; desperately hoping that he was making the right choice this time.

Sarah

Despite her efforts to convince herself that she shouldn't care, Sarah couldn't help feeling nervous as she sat on a black metal bench in Ridgefield Central Park and waited for Benjamin to arrive. She tried to distract herself by watching the vibrant array of fall colors that graced the tops of the trees as they swayed gently in the autumn wind, but her mind was elsewhere. She knew that she was still angry—she had always been one to hold a grudge—but the once-jagged edges of her outrage had somehow softened after Benjamin's confession the night before. Which was strange because she knew herself, and normally she wouldn't have even bothered to listen to someone after they had hurt her like that, but in that moment she realized she had a soft spot for Benjamin that she had never had for anyone else before.

The realization shocked her, and she didn't want to acknowledge it because she was still mad at Benjamin and reeling from the bitter end of her last relationship. The thought of any budding feelings for another man (especially one who had already betrayed her) was something she didn't feel ready for.

So she shook her head of its treacherous thoughts and mentally steeled herself to deal with whatever Benjamin had in store as she straightened her back against the cold metal of the park bench. She glanced down at the watch on her wrist and emotions flooded through her as she remembered who had bought it for her, but she shoved those feelings to the back of her mind and firmly told herself that if he didn't show up soon she wouldn't wait any longer for him. It was already 3:10 p.m.

By 3:15 she was just about to stand up to leave when she felt a tap on her shoulder.

"Now who's the one that's lat—" she said as she turned around to face Benjamin and chide him for being late this time, but she stopped mid-sentence as she laid eyes on the man who stood beside him.

"What is he doing here?" she said, glaring at Oliver as he put his hands in his pockets and sheepishly stared at the ground.

Benjamin's face paled and Sarah wondered why he would expect any other reaction from her. He knew what Oliver had put her through, what did he think would happen? That she wouldn't be mad?

"I was hoping you two could talk; I think there are some things left unsaid and that you both could benefit from finding closure," Benjamin said. He shot her pleading look and Sarah could tell that he desperately wanted this to work, but he should have known better.

"*This* was your big plan? You really think that him and I having a nice little chat will fix all that he did to me, and what *you* did to me?" Sarah said, struggling to keep her voice down as she felt the heat of her anger flush its way into her cheeks.

Now it was Benjamin's turn to stare at the ground. "I just wanted to make things right," he said quietly, and the anguish in his voice seemed to suck some of the anger out of her. She sighed and rubbed her temples in an effort to calm the frustration that swirled inside her mind.

"Look, I'm sorry for reacting like that. I was just a little caught off guard," Sarah admitted.

"I'm sorry, I know I should've given you more heads up but I knew you wouldn't agree to this if I told you," Benjamin said.

Sarah narrowed her eyes and put her hands on her hips. "That's exactly why I'm still upset at you, because you did the same thing with the program. You snuck behind my back because you *knew* that I wasn't going to agree but you did it anyway."

"And *you*," she said, pointing a finger at Oliver, "you know exactly what you did."

Oliver glanced up from the ground and locked eyes with her, his expression full of sorrow and regret. "There is no excuse for what I did Sarah," he began, "and I don't blame you for hating me. What I did was unforgivable and I don't expect you to forgive me, but I do want you to know how sorry I am. There isn't a day that goes by that I don't regret what I did to you and curse myself for losing the best thing that ever happened to me. I'm so, so sorry Sarah, and I just needed to say that to your face."

Sarah stood in stunned silence for a moment as she struggled to process Oliver's heartfelt apology. She had left without a word when she found out and had cut all ties to him so that he had no way of contacting her, so she had no idea that all this time he had been wallowing in remorse and sorrow.

They all stood there for a while, a triangle of hurt and broken bonds that yearned to be mended, and the only sound that filled the air was the delicate whisper of the wind as it rustled the dry leaves on the trees.

"You're right," she said quietly after awhile, not daring to look either of them in the eyes. "I don't know if I can ever forgive you Oliver, but I don't hate you. I wanted to for a long time, but after all we went through together I couldn't seem to shake the place you held in my heart." She looked up at him and saw the pain that she felt mirrored in his eyes. "You and I will never have what we once had, you ruined that forever and it's time for me to move on, but I don't hate you."

She turned to Benjamin, who stared back at her with his soulful amber eyes, and a small smile began to form on her lips. "And you, well, maybe you were right after all. I think this might just work."

She laughed as both of the men in front of her breathed out a visible sigh of relief, feeling a weight lift off her chest that she hadn't been able to free herself from since she had ended things with Oliver.

They spent the next half hour catching up and discussing future plans for Diversity Dawn Academy before the sun dipped behind the trees and the park was cast in a frigid shade that had them tightening their coats around themselves in an effort to keep warm. At that point, they bid Oliver goodbye and Benjamin and Sarah walked to their cars together before stopping in front of Sarah's silver Chevy Malibu.

She smiled as she looked up at him and without thinking wrapped her arms around him in a fond embrace. He froze in shock for a second before wrapping his arms around her in response. They stood there for only a moment, but it felt right somehow—like they fit together perfectly.

"Thank you," Benjamin said as they pulled apart from each other, and Sarah smiled up at him.

"Thank you for doing that," she said. "But don't ever go behind my back again."

Benjamin chuckled. "Trust me, I learned my lesson. I'm going to do everything I can to make sure that temper of yours is only ever directed at Evan Peters and not me."

Sarah whacked him gently across the arm. "I do *not* have a temper."

"Uh-huh. Tell that to my nightmares."

Sarah threw her head back and laughed freely, feeling more at ease than she had in a long time. Benjamin chuckled before opening her car door for her, and Sarah hopped in her driver's seat.

"See you Monday," Benjamin said.

"See you then Ben," Sarah said, closing her car door and starting her engine. Benjamin beamed at her before turning and walking towards his own car, and Sarah smiled as she realized just how relieved she was that everything was back to normal.

Chapter 8:

A Guiding Hand

Benjamin

After having conquered the hurdles that Benjamin and Sarah had to jump through to keep the program alive, they decided that they would waste no more time. They shifted their focus back to their students and the alternative education model that they were uniquely fine-tuning to suit their students' needs.

In an effort to deepen their educational experience, the staff at Diversity Dawn Academy carefully integrated project-based learning into their curriculum and introduced it to the students as a method to express their interests in the real-world applications of their studies.

For English, Sarah guided her students through the process of creating New Horizon's very own newspaper, and for math Benjamin had his students work through and master basic problems in probability by researching certain topics that apply to their interests and concerns (such as driving and cell phone use or the costs associated with a college education) and explaining how probability affects said aspect of their lives.

For science, Ms. Honey taught her students about biology by facilitating a community garden that served to support a local soup kitchen, and for PE Mrs. Laurence helped her students create a personalized workout plan that was suited to their specific physical needs.

Mr. Gilbert, the social studies teacher, decided to take his class on a field trip to a local history museum as his way of introducing project-based learning. Benjamin and Sarah fully supported this idea and decided to come along as extra help so that they could split the class into groups.

And so there they were at the Ridgefield Historical Museum, where Maria, Jamal, and Alex were finding the trip especially enlightening. Maria had always loved the history and culture that museums were drenched in. As someone with direct origins to a different country, it was very intriguing to study the history and customs of the country you live in and compare the differences to the country your roots came from.

For Jamal, he found the museum trip interesting because it gave him a chance to explore the historical injustices that were prevalent in almost every narrative he came across. It made him hungry for change and motivated to make a difference.

Alex loved the museum because she loved art. She considered herself a budding artist, and she found herself getting lost in the various art styles that adorned the walls of the museum. She loved to experiment, but her favorite art medium was oil paints so she was particularly fascinated by the oil paintings that she discovered that day.

The students left the museum feeling inspired and invigorated, and even spurred on by the museum visitors who they caught smiling as they watched the students become enraptured by the museum and its treasures.

***

Benjamin and Sarah saw the potential in every one of their students and recognized how beneficial a mentorship program could be because, while they all did very well during their project-based learning projects, the staff realized that their students could all find support from being paired with community leaders who share similar interests or backgrounds.

So they set to work facilitating the mentorship program by reaching out to the community and proposing the idea to them. They weren't entirely sure if it would work out, but to their surprise the community response was overwhelmingly positive. They had more than enough people volunteer to devote their time to mentoring students, so they had each student and each mentor fill out a questionnaire that would help create accurate and beneficial pairs.

Maria was paired with Angelica Elvira, an immigrant rights advocate who helped her recognize that she was not the only one who suffered from the debilitating effects of the looming threat of deportation, and that there were steps she and her family could take to resolve the issue and live without that storm cloud darkening their lives.

Reggie Stevens, a businessman who ran the local grocery store and championed diversity, became a mentor for Jamal. Through him, Jamal learned that racism is not something to sit back and tolerate, and that he must stand up for himself and embrace his culture and heritage with open and loving arms.

Alex found a mentor in Liz Rose, an LGBTQ+ community organizer who helped her realize that she had nothing to be ashamed of and that she was most definitely not a freak. Instead, she was part of a vibrant, thriving community that loved and supported her, and Alex found herself embracing her sexuality and letting her true self shine without inhibitions or fear of judgment.

Sarah and Benjamin were filled with pride and joy as they watched their students grow and thrive under the guiding hands of their mentors and through utilizing the support and resources that Diversity Dawn Academy eagerly offered them. They found themselves feeling accomplished and ready for the next challenge that might come their way, so they decided that improving their relationships with the students' parents was the next task at hand. The staff collectively planned a Parent's Night and invited each and every one of Diversity Dawn Academy's students and their families to join them for a chance to showcase their growth and progress. It didn't take long for the night to arrive, and Benjamin and Sarah felt their excitement (and anxiety) rise as more and more parents and students arrived at the community center where they held the meet and greet before the school year even started.

It felt like so long ago that they had met these students and their parents, because so much had changed since that point. They were so excited to share the students' progress with the parents and showcase how much they'd grown and flourished under the stable wings of the program.

Maria

Maria left Parent's Night with her family feeling lighter and more full of hope than she had in a long time. It had taken rigorous effort on her part to convince her parents and grandparents to even consider letting her enroll in Diversity Dawn Academy—never mind to make a physical appearance at the program—and she was proud of herself for bringing them out of their shells. She knew the threat of deportation that loomed over their heads was still very real, but it had felt so empowering to show her grandparents that such a small thing like showing up at your grandchild's school was not going to immediately result in ICE knocking down their door.

She lay in her bed that night feeling like a weight had lifted off of her chest, and her heart was so full of hope for the future that she even considered asking her grandparents how they would feel about letting her play the violin at school now. With a yawn, she smiled to herself and drifted off to sleep where she dreamed of a bright future that awaited her.

When she woke up the next morning, however, she felt the familiar heaviness of dread settle itself on her chest and she frowned as she tried to figure out why an impending sense of doom followed her every thought.

She tried to shake the feeling that something was off throughout the rest of her day, but it plagued her like a bird of prey that had hooked its talons in her mind. By the time lunch rolled around, Maria knew something was up. She spent her last classes feeling distracted as she struggled to figure out what could be wrong, but it wasn't until she arrived home and saw the anguish and terror on her mother's face that the pieces fit into place.

"What happened?" she asked her mother, discarding her school bag to the floor as she closed the distance between them. As she did, she caught the distinct sheen of tears in her mother's eyes and her heart plummeted as she desperately hoped that her mind was just jumping to conclusions and what she feared hadn't happened.

"I don't know how, I don't know who, but somehow someone found out," her mother said, her voice quivering with emotion. "We got the deportation notice this morning after you left for school."

Maria felt her world fall apart around her as she realized that the thing she feared the most, the nightmare that had plagued her dreams she was old enough to understand the threat of deportation, had come true.

"It's all my fault, they didn't want to go to Parent's Night and I made them, I did this..." she said, choking on the tears that welled in her own eyes.

"No mija, don't blame yourself. We don't know that it was Parent's Night that brought this on," her mother said gently, reaching out to embrace her daughter.

Maria took a step back and shook her head as she felt her tears start to flow freely. "I'm so sorry," she whispered, hanging her head and staring at the floor.

"Mija..." her mother said, and the heartbreak in her voice sent Maria spiraling.

"I will fix this," Maria said firmly, looking up from the floor and staring into her mother's eyes, "I promise."

"Maria wait!" her mother called after her as she turned to leave, but Maria knew exactly where she had to go—the one place where she knew she could find support.

***

"I'm so sorry Maria," Ms. Mitchell said, and Maria could tell from the genuine concern that filled the English teacher's eyes that she really meant it.

Mr. Diamonds shook his head from where he stood beside Ms. Mitchell, and Maria could practically see the gears whirring in his brain as he began to pace manically across the room in an effort to brainstorm potential courses of action.

They were seated in the staff room at Diversity Dawn Academy, and Alex sat beside her holding her hand. They had grown quite close over the last couple months, and she was the only person she thought to call as she made her way over to the program, knowing that Mr. Diamonds and Ms. Mitchell would probably still be there wrapping up before heading home.

"First, we need to rally the community so we can implement a support system for your family, and then we'll set to work on organizing legal assistance so that we can do everything in our power to stop them from being deported," Mr. Diamond said firmly, the lines in his forehead creasing with concern.

"Thank you," Maria croaked out, struggling to hold back the tears that brimmed in her eyes. Alex squeezed her hand and smiled gently at her, her gaze full of compassion and sympathy.

"We're not going to let this happen without a fight," she said.

As heavy as her heart was with the thought of never seeing her grandparents again, she also felt the warmth of gratitude swell inside her chest as she realized that she didn't know what she would do if she hadn't signed up for Diversity Dawn Academy and found such a strong support system to help her through this.

Chapter 9:

Advocating for Change

Jamal

Jamal's heart was heavy as his mind filled with thoughts of Maria and her family. He considered her a close friend after getting to know her through the program, and the news of her family's struggle with deportation hit him hard. He was so enraged by the unfairness of it all, and the fact that he felt helpless to do anything about it made it even worse. He aimlessly kicked the pebbles on the sidewalk as he shuffled his way home, feeling distraught and wishing there was some way he could help Maria and others who suffer from the same injustice.

He was so preoccupied with his own thoughts that he didn't pay any mind to the police officer who was eyeing him suspiciously from across the street. He was used to discrimination because of the color of his skin, and on a day like today he did his best to not let it affect him. He was furious enough at the injustice of Maria's grandparents' deportation notice, and he didn't need more inequity to fuel his exasperation at the unfairness of the world.

So he kept his head down and quickened his pace in an effort to escape the critical gaze of the police officer through his aviator-style sunglasses. Something about him made Jamal think that he looked like the kind of cop who sought out trouble just because he was bored, and Jamal knew better than to catch the eye of a policeman like that.

Just as he was about to turn the corner and leave the scrutiny of the police officer's eyes, Jamal was caught off guard as the man suddenly appeared in front of him with a feral grin on his face.

"Where do you think you're going?" the officer said as he stuck his arm out and leaned on the building beside them, blocking Jamal from passing through.

"I'm going home," Jamal muttered, refusing to look the man in the eyes and instead glowering at the ground.

"You looked pretty suspicious running away from me like that, you got anything to hide?" he said, his smile shifting from feral to wicked.

"I wasn't running," Jamal insisted with a scowl, still staring at the ground.

"Sure looked like you were," the officer replied, "and now you won't even look me in the eyes."

"Well I wasn't," Jamal shot back, feeling his anger rise as he stared up defiantly at the police officer. This was the last thing he needed today.

The man's grin disappeared off his face and his eyes darkened. With pasty white skin and shrewd beady eyes, the man wasn't pretty to begin with, and the sneer that slowly formed to twist up his features made him seem even more menacing.

"I don't like your attitude, *boy*, and someone by the likes of you has obviously got something to hide," he spat, glancing up and down at Jamal.

Jamal bristled as he realized exactly what the man was insinuating: he better shut his mouth and take the shit that was dolled out to him because he was Black and therefore obviously a criminal. Jamal had just about enough of injustice today, and he wasn't about to stand here and take more from some man who thought he could belittle him just because his skin was dark.

"I have nothing to hide," he said, glaring up into the man's beady green eyes, "and I'm going home now." He shoved his way past the officer and stomped down the street, bracing for the outrage that he knew was coming.

It didn't take long before he felt the meaty hand of the officer clamp down on his shoulder, and Jamal struggled to avoid stumbling to the ground as he was spun around roughly.

"Where do you think you're going?" the man repeated, his voice barely above a growl. His fingernails dug into Jamal's shoulder and he had shoved his face so close that Jamal swore he could smell the stench of alcohol on his breath.

Jamal knew he was in trouble now. Still, he couldn't seem to rein in his temper and force himself to perform the sniveling compliance act that he knew the officer wanted from him.

"Let me go!" he yelled as the man's nails dug deeper into his shoulder, cutting into his flesh through his shirt.

"Fat chance kid, you're coming with me," the officer said with a devilish grin as he yanked Jamal down the street towards his cruiser.

Jamal felt the icy tendrils of dread grip his heart as he realized what he had just gotten himself into. *Looks like Maria's grandparents aren't the only ones in trouble with the law now*, he thought to himself grimly as he was brutally shoved into the back of a cop car.

Benjamin

Benjamin couldn't seem to stop his hands from shaking as he hung up his phone. In the frenzy of desperately trying to support Maria and her family, he was already feeling overwhelmed by his emotions but the phone call he just had with Jamal's mother sent him over the edge. He sank his head in his hands as he reeled from the devastating news that he had yet to fully process, but he knew he didn't have time to wallow in his anguish—he needed to be a steady pillar of support for his students to rely on. So he took a shaky deep breath in and stood up straight, letting his hands fall to his sides as he strode quickly forward to find Sarah. He had to find her so they could figure out what their next steps were.

Benjamin felt his heart tighten as he watched Sarah's smile falter when she saw the look on his face, and he desperately wished he wasn't about to deliver even more bad news. He watched as the color drained from Sarah's face after telling her that Jamal had been arrested and an uncomfortable silence filled the room as they took a moment for the severity of the situation to sink in.

"We need to get him out of there," Sarah said, her face grim with determination.

Benjamin nodded solemnly. "We will, I'm not going to let him rot in there when I know he's a good kid with a bright future. There's no way I'm going to let them take that away from him."

Alex

The days following Jamal's wrongful arrest were filled with a whirlwind of activity at Diversity Dawn Academy. They all focused on collectively organizing legal aid and using the social injustices that Maria and Jamal were suffering from as a catalyst for an in-depth conversation within the program; a teachable moment where the educators addressed civil rights and the importance of advocacy with their students.

Alex grappled with her emotions as she navigated the tense waters of Diversity Dawn Academy and worried for her friends. But even with all the stress that filled the classrooms, Alex felt much more comfortable at the alternative education program than she had at Ridgefield High. There were no bullies at Diversity Dawn Academy, although Brody was a bit of a jerk, but that was nothing compared to what she had to deal with in her old classes.

She had to admit that leaving Veronica and her flunkies behind was one of the best decisions that she had ever made, and her grades were evidence of that. Now that she didn't have to deal with "misplaced" notes and judgmental teachers, her grades were finally matching the dedication and effort she put into them.

Alex was just starting to feel hopeful for the first time since she came out, she and Maria had become close friends and it even seemed like her parents were starting to realize that she wasn't just making up excuses about the bullying now that they could see her flourishing in a new school environment. Everything felt like it was falling into place—until Maria's grandparents got a deportation notice and Jamal got detained when he should've been left alone.

These injustices weighed heavily on Alex's heart as she walked home from school after a day that had been full of futile advancements to right the wrongs that her classmates were experiencing. It felt like life couldn't get any worse at that moment, but when she suddenly caught sight of the familiar shine of blonde hair in front of her, she realized that it could.

"Hey freak, heard you started the new year at school for 'special' kids," Veronica teased mercilessly as she approached Alex, her gang of bullies flocking beside her.

"We always knew you needed extra help, poor freak can't do things right without her special school," one of Veronica's friends said, a fake pout pursed on her lips.

"It's for *marginalized* students, which I wouldn't be if people like you weren't so ignorant and afraid of people who are different from them," Alex said vehemently, feeling more confident now that she knew what it felt like to have a support system.

Veronica blinked in surprise before she shrugged nonchalantly. A cruel smile slowly spread across her face and she opened her mouth to spit out the poison that dripped from her lips. "Whatever you have to tell yourself to feel better about the fact that you're stupid and don't fit in, *freak*."

"I'm not a freak!" Alex yelled, feeling frustrated with all the injustice that her world was full of already. She knew she didn't deserve to be treated like this, Diversity Dawn Academy had taught her that she was more than what these bullies thought she was.

"Ouu the freak is feeling feisty today, are you upset about your little girlfriend's grandparents getting sent back to where they belong?" Veronica spat, her eyes gleaming with the vicious fire of pure hatred.

Alex was taken aback for a moment. *How did she know about Maria?*

As if sensing her thoughts, the blonde bully smiled wickedly in triumph. "We know all about your little girlfriend and her illegal parents. My cousin saw them at Parent's Night and she heard her parents whispering about illegal immigrants. Next thing we knew, all of a sudden her grandparents got a deportation notice, whoops!"

Alex felt the cloud of rage blur her vision as she realized what Veronica had just confessed. *How dare she?* Alex seethed to herself. *Bullying is one thing, but messing with people's lives and futures is disgusting.*

"Oh does that make the little freak upset?" Veronica said in a sugar-sweet voice that was laced with contempt. "Too bad there's nothing you can do about it."

Alex squeezed her eyes shut as she tried to drown out the voices that taunted her and threatened to throw her over the edge of controlling her anger. She knew they were just trying to get a reaction out of her, and she wasn't about to give them that satisfaction.

So she opened her eyes and shoved her earbuds in, blasting her music loud enough so that she couldn't hear the putrid words that spewed from Veronica's mouth. Then she pushed past the bullies without another word, determined to ignore them and make her way home so she could process the events of the day without being judged by the cruel girls.

She didn't turn back and instead walked briskly down the street, hoping that Veronica and her tribe of bullies weren't ruthless enough to follow her.

These were the girls who had been bullying her mercilessly for as long as she could remember though, so she should have known better.

Alex felt the air suddenly leave her lungs as she was remorselessly shoved onto the cold hard pavement of the sidewalk. She cried out as she realized her hands were being held behind her back and couldn't use them to catch herself. She landed on her chin with a brutal thud that shook her teeth and rattled her brain, and suddenly the metallic taste of blood filled her mouth.

"Holy shit Veronica," she heard one of the bullies say from behind her, obviously in shock.

"Let's get out of here," Veronica said, and the next thing Alex heard was the sound of their footsteps as they ran away, leaving her in a pool of her own blood on the sidewalk.

Benjamin

The attack on Alex just blocks from Ridgefield High was the last straw. Sarah and Benjamin responded by immediately organizing an emergency meeting with the school board to implement comprehensive anti-bullying policies and demand improved protection for all students, but especially marginalized ones who were more likely to become victims of bullying.

After getting in touch with legal assistance in an effort to get him released as soon as possible, Benjamin and Sarah also rallied a network of community advocates for Jamal during the aftermath of his arrest by organizing community meetings to rally support and raise awareness of the negative effect of racial discrimination.

Recognizing that the effects of recent events were affecting their students' mental health and stability, Benjamin and Sarah facilitated a series of workshops to address these concerns and provide emotional support in an effort to avoid having grades affected by the stress and tension of the situation.

They also decided to hold a school-wide assembly on discrimination in an effort to provide a platform for students to share their own experiences with discrimination and injustice so they can validate their feelings. On the night of the assembly, Benjamin looked out across the sea of young faces that stared down at him from their seats on Ridgefield High's bleachers and took a deep breath as he began his speech from where he stood on a makeshift podium in the grass of the football field.

"Nobody deserves to feel like they are less than someone else. We are all human; all just people who really aren't much different from each other. We all breathe the same air and live in the same world, yet some people have skewed perspectives of others that make it difficult for them to understand how similar we all are. These skewed perceptions and beliefs stem from ignorance, and ignorance can fester and breed in the dark if we don't shine a light on it," Benjamin said, smiling sadly at the students in front of him.

"So that's why we are gathered here tonight, because the ruthless wrath of ignorance has negatively affected a number of our very own students in extremely harmful ways. We are here tonight to shine a light on ignorance by informing ourselves of the dangers of discrimination. So please, open your hearts and let the light of these stories you hear tonight shine on the darkness that surrounds you."

Benjamin stepped down from the podium and smiled at Maria who nervously took his place, her hands shaking as she held her note cards in front of her.

"My family has always had a storm cloud, one that hung over our heads at all times," she began timidly, her voice steadying with confidence as she continued. "That storm cloud was the threat of deportation, because my grandparents are undocumented immigrants."

Benjamin could tell from the way her voice shook that saying that out loud must have been really hard for her, but he also knew it must've been slightly therapeutic to finally let the weight of that secret off her chest.

"Growing up, I was never allowed to draw publicity to myself or my family in any way—whether it was good or bad. That meant that I was never allowed to play my violin the way I wanted to, at least not in public, because the fear that it might draw attention always loomed over my head. I grew up marginalized and constantly in fear because of the discrimination that fueled a hatred for illegal immigrants, and I'm here tonight to share my story so that others who have suffered as I have can know that they are not alone."

With that, she stepped down from the podium, standing taller than Benjamin had even seen her stand.

"You did amazing, your grandparents would be proud," he told her, and she smiled back with the sheen of tears in her eyes.

Next Sarah walked up to the podium with a sheet of paper in her hands.

"Since Jamal unfortunately can't join us right now, he wrote this and asked that I share it tonight," she said sadly.

"I have always been treated differently," Sarah began as she read the words on the paper. "Even though my mother always did her best to protect me, I grew up knowing that I was never going to be treated the same as my classmates with lighter skin. I never understood why—I still don't—but I know it to be true. Just last June I applied to a poetry contest online and almost won, until I told them what my name was and they realized that I was Black. That's what led me to the doors of Diversity Dawn Academy, where I have learned that I should be proud of my heritage and stand up for my rights. And that's exactly what I did one day when I was walking home from school and a police officer stopped me for no reason other than the color of my skin. I tried to walk away, but he threw me in his cruiser and told me I was up to no good 'because of who I am.' I am writing this to shine a light on the darkness that discrimination can cast on the lives of those who are different, and to tell them that no matter what color their skin is, they don't deserve to be treated unfairly."

Sarah looked up at the crowd for a moment after finishing to let Jamal's words sink in before she stepped down from the podium and turned to Alex beside her, whose face was still swollen and bruised.

Alex stepped up to the podium with no note cards or paper to guide her, and Benjamin admired the fact that she chose to speak from her heart.

"Nobody believed me when I told them that I was being bullied. When I cried and begged and pleaded for help they all just thought I was asking for special privileges because I identify as bisexual. Nobody gave me the time of day to listen to my concerns, most people wouldn't even look at me—like I was such a disappointment and they were so disgusted by my existence that they couldn't stand the sight of me." Alex glared defiantly at the students in front of her, and Benjamin felt pride surge in his chest for her bravery. He couldn't imagine how hard it must be for her to confront her bullies and be so vulnerable in front of the whole school.

"It wasn't until I came home covered in blood after being *attacked* that people finally started to realize that I wasn't making it up, that I was being bullied and I was scared for my safety—all because of the way I dress and the fact that I identify as LGBTQ+, because I'm different and people can't accept that. They're so scared of change that they want to punish me for being who I am." Alex's hands shook from the anger that must have been coursing through her veins.

"I'm here tonight to share my story in the hopes that people will understand that ignorance and discrimination leads to bullying, and that the cries of a victim should *never* be ignored." With that, she stepped down from the podium and retreated to her place beside Maria, who hugged her tightly.

The words of Maria, Jamal, and Alex even inspired a few more students to step up to the podium and share their own stories, and Benjamin felt a small smile tug his lips as his heart filled with pride for his students, students who were brave enough to share their stories so that they could advocate for the change that this world so desperately needed.

After everyone who wanted to had a chance to share their personal experiences with discrimination, Benjamin and Sarah asked that everyone please purchase a candle to reinforce the concept of bringing light to the darkness of discrimination and injustice so that the proceeds could go toward supporting Jamal's and Maria's grandparents' legal aid.

To their surprise, they actually ran out of candles to sell and made much more than they were expecting to, which was excellent because their limited budget was struggling to afford the legal assistance that they had hired.

As the school football field lit up with dozens upon dozens of candles, Benjamin found himself reaching out to Sarah beside him and squeezing her hand as his heart slowly filled with the warm sense of hope.

Chapter 10:

The Winter Concert

Maria

In the weeks that followed the discrimination awareness assembly, the proceeds that Diversity Dawn Academy had gathered from candle sales had turned the tide for the legal aid that opposed Jamal's wrongful arrest and Maria's grandparents' deportation notice. After fierce legal battles that shook the foundations of Diversity Dawn Academy to its very core and left Benjamin and Sarah reeling from the effort they had to put into securing justice, Jamal returned home soon after the assembly and Maria's grandparents were granted the chance to attempt to become American citizens by applying for Green Cards.

Benjamin and Sarah knew that the students deserved a chance to recover after the traumatic events that had unfolded before them in the last couple weeks, so they proposed that they throw an event of some sort to celebrate their newfound victory.

After much deliberation and debate, it was collectively decided that they should organize a concert since Maria didn't have to hide her talent for the violin anymore and she was eager to musically express herself from outside the confines of her home after all that she had just overcome. So she was entrusted with the honor of creating Diversity Dawn Academy's very own anthem and asked to play it at the Winter Concert. She spent weeks preparing and perfecting the anthem, and Benjamin and Sarah insisted that she keep it a surprise for the concert, knowing that whatever she created would be exactly the anthem that Diversity Dawn Academy needed to live by.

Alex was also asked to create an art piece blended with Jamal's talent for poetry so that they could finally showcase their talents without the shadow of discrimination darkening the art they longed to create. Other students from Diversity Dawn Academy were encouraged to share their talents as well so that every student felt included and was given a chance to shine as brightly as they could.

When the night of the concert finally came, the air in Ridgefield High's gymnasium was charged with anticipation and hushed whispers as the crowd eagerly awaited the chance to hear the Diversity Dawn Academy anthem for the first time.

Maria tentatively emerged onto the stage as the lights dimmed in preparation for her performance. After waiting so long for the chance to play in public and not have to hide her talent away, she couldn't help but notice the beads of sweat that dripped across her brow from the nerves that threatened to overcome her. She had never stood on a stage before—had never been given the chance to—and now that she was, the feeling of so many eyes on her at once became so overwhelming that her chest tightened from the heavy weight of anxiety settling on her like a dark storm cloud.

Her eyes frantically roved over the crowd that sat expectantly in front of her, and she felt as if the walls were closing in on her as panic hit in the full force of its brutality. People started to whisper and frown as they realized that she hadn't taken a step forward since she walked onto the stage, and it wasn't until a pair of bright green eyes set among a sea of freckles locked onto her own that she felt herself release a breath she hadn't released she'd been holding. Alex smiled and gave her a gentle nod of encouragement, silently reminding Maria that she was done with feeling trapped under storm clouds. Maria smiled back at her gratefully before taking a deep breath to steady her nerves and stepping into the spotlight at the center of the stage.

The light blinded her for a moment, but as soon as her eyes adjusted she smiled at the crowd, no longer feeling the weight of the storm cloud over her head.

"When I found out that my grandparents had received a deportation notice, it felt as if my world crumbled beneath my feet. I had spent my entire life cowering under the fear of that possibility and my whole family did everything they possibly could to avoid it from happening.

But my time at Diversity Dawn Academy has taught me that secrets never stay in the dark, like all things in life they will eventually be brought to the light—and maybe that's a good thing. If my grandparents had never gotten that deportation notice then nothing would have changed, they would have lived in fear for the rest of their lives. *I* would have lived in fear for the rest of their lives, and that is a horrible way to live."

Maria paused to let her words sink in before continuing, "The hardest part about writing this anthem for Diversity Dawn Academy was coming up with a title, a meaning to the melody that flowed through me. But as soon as I did I realized it had been staring at me for as long as I have been a part of Diversity Dawn Academy. This anthem is called '*The Light in the Darkness*,' and it represents the beacon of hope that this program has brought to my life. It is my hope that the notes I play for you all tonight can inspire others to join Diversity Dawn Academy; others who could use a little light in their life."

Maria took a steadying breath after finishing her speech and brought her violin up to her shoulder, clamping it with her chin and resting her bow against the strings for a moment as she prepared herself. Then she closed her eyes and let the melody flow through her like it had when she first created it. All she had to do was think of the days she'd spent at Diversity Dawn Academy, of the faces that she'd met there and the light of hope that hovers around the entire program and it was like her hand took over as it gently caressed the strings of her violin with her bow and music poured out from the stage like a river of sound.

When she opened her eyes, she looked to the mural set in front of her on the back wall of the gymnasium and watched as it seemed to light up from the notes that swirled around the room. The vibrant colors of the intertwined roots and interconnected hands under the vivid oil painting of a sun peeking over a green horizon shone brightly before her and encouraged her to play even louder, filling the gymnasium with the heartfelt notes that she hoped conveyed the hope and resilience and love for Diversity Dawn Academy that filled her chest as she played them. She knew the words written by Jamal's hand that stood underneath the mural spoke of the resilient nature of hope, of the light that shines even in the darkest of places, and the promise of a bright future that a new dawn can hold and she smiled as she felt pride swell in her chest for the glorious mural that her friends had created—a symbol of hope and strength in the face of adversity.

For Maria, the anthem was timeless, and she had no idea how long she had been playing before her final note rang out into the air and she gently brought her violin to her side, looking out into the crowd to see the universality of emotion and understanding displayed in the faces that peered up at her. In the next instant, the air erupted with the fervent applause of the audience and Maria found Alex's face as she whooped and hollered excitedly for Maria's performance.

A single tear slid down Maria's face as she finally felt the warmth of the light that the storm cloud of fear had blocked her from relishing in until this moment, and she was filled with gratitude for the program that had made it all possible.

Chapter 11:

Leaders Are Born Every Day

Kaylee

After all that they had been through together, Kaylee felt that Maria, Jamal, Alex, and her were closer now than ever before. Maria and Alex had become practically inseparable and Jamal and Kaylee had made their relationship official pretty much as soon as Jamal was released. The group found themselves bonding over their shared experiences and love of Diversity Dawn Academy one day in the local pizza shop after school.

"I don't want to think about what my life would be like right now if I hadn't signed up for Diversity Dawn Academy," Alex said thoughtfully as she stared out of the window beside her. She was seated beside Maria in the faded red leather booth that the group had come to frequent when they weren't at school. Jamal and Kaylee were comfortably cuddled up against each other on the other side of the booth and the familiar aroma of marinara and sizzling cheese filled the air between them all as they reflected on how life-changing their time at Diversity Dawn Academy had been.

The others voiced the fact that they could all relate to Alex's statement, and their hearts filled with gratitude for the support they received from the outstretched wings of the program who had been there for them through each of their personal hardships.

"It's sad that not everyone has such a solid support system to advocate for them and uplift them during hard times," Kaylee said with a sigh as she laid her head on Jamal's shoulder.

"Yeah, there needs to be more support systems out there for marginalized students," Maria agreed with a solemn nod.

Jamal's brow furrowed in thought as he considered his friend's words. "Why don't we make some then?"

Alex raised an eyebrow in confusion at him from across the table. "What do you mean 'make them?'"

"I mean just that, let's use what we've learned from Diversity Dawn Academy and the strength that we've gained from overcoming our personal hardships to help other students like us who don't have the support we do. Let's be their support and make our own effort to change things," Jamal said excitedly, his face lighting up with the passion that supported his words.

The three girls shared eager smiles as the meaning of Jamal's idea sunk in. "Let's do it," they said in unison.

***

The group of friends immediately set to work on bringing their plan to life by individually taking the lead on initiatives that aimed to tackle the social injustices they each personally faced. In doing so, their hearts sang with the hopeful song of fulfillment as they turned their struggles into pathways for others to overcome their hardships just like the students of Diversity Dawn Academy did. By spreading awareness and promoting advocacy, the four friends felt themselves become a part of something bigger, something that felt as bright and as promising as the light that Diversity Dawn Academy had brought into their lives.

Maria spearheaded a fundraising campaign to support the ongoing legal battle surrounding the immigration rights that her grandparents deserved to be respected with and also focused on spreading awareness of the struggles that immigrants often face. Kaylee was inspired by her emerging leadership skills that shone brightly as she fought tooth and nail to help her grandparents in the best way she knew how to.

Now that Jamal had firsthand experience with racial profiling, he was more adamant than ever before to help make sure that nobody else had to suffer through what he did. So, in a daring and inspiring move, he partnered with local law enforcement to organize workshops that he hoped would help foster mutual respect and understanding within the community. Kaylee's feelings for him deepened even further as he positioned himself as a key youth advocate in the community by taking action to help diminish racial profiling.

Still shaken from the attack that left her physically damaged, Alex takes the initiative to launch an inclusivity campaign within Diversity Dawn Academy and Ridgefield High that not only established a safe space for LGBTQ+ students but also raised awareness of the dangers of bullying and ignorance by fostering acceptance and empowerment. Kaylee knew how critical that was for the students who needed that support, and she was proud of her friend for being brave enough to take on such a challenge.

The pride in Kaylee's chest swelled even more when Mr. Diamonds and Ms. Mitchell announced that Diversity Dawn Academy was going to host an open house that would showcase the incredible work that their students were doing and the growth that they had all undertaken since stepping into the classrooms of the alternative education program.

Benjamin

The planning and organizing of the open house became a collaborative effort between the teachers and students of Diversity Dawn Academy—and even volunteers from the community who were so invested in the program that they wanted to help showcase its success. They all spent weeks making sure that every last detail was meticulously prepared for, because they understood the significance of the event and the potential it held to exhibit the transformative power of alternative education.

When the day of the open house finally arrived, the excitement and nerves that hung in the air were almost tangible. Benjamin felt them mirrored in his own feelings of simultaneously worrying about what might go wrong and being ecstatic about the chance to show off the program that he devoted all of his recent time and energy to, which was something he planned to continue doing so for the foreseeable future.

As usual, Sarah was there to calm him down, and he was more grateful than ever that they had worked through their personal struggles and stood side by side again. With all the turmoil that the program had faced recently, they hadn't had a chance to revive the feelings that had sparked and danced under the moonlight on their date that seemed so long ago, but now that the dust had started to settle, Benjamin allowed himself to let those feelings flourish inside him again.

He sent her a smile that he hoped conveyed those feelings to Sarah as they stood across the room waiting for the open house guests to arrive, and the blush that crept into her cheeks as she smiled shyly back at him told him all he needed to know.

Benjamin was suddenly overwhelmed with the impulsive urge to cross the room and confess his feelings to the educator that had been there for him since they joined paths, but fortunately the open house guests arrived before he could do such a brazen thing.

He shook his head subtly and smiled to himself as he brought his focus back to the open house and the chance to showcase Diversity Dawn Academy. It was an important day for the program and its members, and Benjamin knew it wasn't the time to explore his feelings for Sarah right now.

So he turned to watch his students smile and greet the guests and felt his chest fill with pride for the adolescents who had taken it upon themselves to help make the world a better place for marginalized students like themselves.

Much like at the discrimination assembly, some of the students had prepared speeches to elaborate on the growth and support that they have experienced at Diversity Dawn Academy and to showcase its unique approach to alternative education.

Maria stepped up to the microphone first, and she seemed much more sure of herself than she had when she stood in front of Ridgefield High on the bleachers at the discrimination assembly. An air of confidence surrounded her, and her warm smile made the guests feel at ease and eager to hear what she had to say.

"Before I joined Diversity Dawn Academy, I was struggling to find myself amidst the dark storm cloud that constantly loomed over my head. My grandparents were illegal immigrants, and the incessant fear of deportation was always with me; a sickening feeling in my gut that I just couldn't seem to shake off no matter what I did. I had to blend into the background and was unable to fully express my talent and love for playing the violin in order to avoid drawing attention to myself and my family. I felt hopeless, like there was a darkness hovering over my life that I thought would never leave." Maria's eyes grew dark as she remembered that time in her life before she smiled sadly and continued her story.

"That's when I saw a flyer for Diversity Dawn Academy at the community center, and since that moment everything has changed. Because of this program, my grandparents are on track to receiving their Green Cards, and that dark storm cloud is finally clearing away to review a new dawn that looks brighter than I ever could have imagined. I don't feel hopeless anymore now, I feel excited for the future that Diversity Dawn Academy has helped make possible," Maria said with a grin that lit up the room.

"And so, Diversity Dawn Academy has provided me with the resources and confidence to fight against the injustice that my grandparents are currently struggling with by initiating a fundraising campaign to help support the ongoing legal battle that they have been caught up in for the last month. Without this program, none of it would be possible."

The resounding sound of applause filled the air as Maria stepped back from the microphone and made room for Jamal to take her place. He stood proudly in front of the crowd with a wide grin on his face as he waited for the clapping to die down so he could begin his speech.

"If it wasn't for Diversity Dawn Academy, I wouldn't be standing here today. It's more than likely that I would be locked up for simply being who I am and not conforming to the oppression of racism. For those of you who don't know, I was arrested last month because I 'looked suspicious,' and as upsetting an example of discrimination and racism that it was, it did provide me with the chance to meet my father." Jamal paused for a moment to let his words sink in before continuing.

"Growing up, my dad had never been a part of the picture and my mom always dodged my questions when I asked why. It wasn't until I met him in detention that I realized why she shielded me from the truth. My father was arrested on a similar charge, and while the details weren't exactly the same, the reason behind them was—racism. I lived out my childhood without a father because of a case of mistaken identity, and the court system forced him to plead guilty to a crime he didn't commit. The worst part is that if it wasn't for the support and advocacy that Diversity Dawn Academy extended to me, I would be in there with him right now." Jamal took a deep breath in to steady himself.

"After experiencing the devastating effects of discrimination firsthand, I made the decision to take it upon myself to help others avoid the same fate by hosting workshops in collaboration with my local police force that spread awareness and foster mutual understanding and respect. By doing so, it is my hope that I can uplift my community members from the haunting burden that discrimination can have on our lives."

Another round of deafening applause filled the room as Jamal finished his speech and Alex stepped forward to begin her own. She stood tall in front of the microphone, her face resolute as she looked out at the crowd that sat in front of her.

"Without this program, I wouldn't have the confidence or experience to advocate for others who still suffer from the nightmares that I once suffered silently through. Before I joined Diversity Dawn Academy, I was struggling to achieve decent grades at Ridgefield High. This wasn't because I didn't try enough or wasn't smart enough, it was because I had recently come out as bisexual and a trio of girls in my peer group took it upon themselves to make my life miserable because of it. They stole my homework, flushed my notes down the toilet, poised the teachers and staff against me, and even physically attacked me." Alex turned her face slightly to showcase the faint scar that was still healing on her bottom lip.

"After yet another teacher refused to believe me when I insisted that it wasn't my fault that I had failed a test, I realized that I never wanted to be treated the way I was treated at Ridgefield High ever again. So I dove into research in an effort to find a new school that would support me, or at least not tear me down for being different. Diversity Dawn Academy became my haven, and my time there has inspired me to help others like myself navigate the troubled waters of self-acceptance and find the support they deserve. So I launched an inclusivity campaign within Ridgefield High that provides a safe place for LGBTQ+ students and includes activities and programs which aim to raise awareness of the drastic effects of bullying and discrimination can have on marginalized students."

Alex stepped back to stand with Jamal and Maria, and the trio received a standing ovation for their speeches. Benjamin stood beside Sarah and together they watched their students receive the adulation they so completely deserved, and he felt his chest swell with the full feeling of pride and gratitude that had become familiar in the last couple months that Diversity Dawn Academy had been soaring through.

The rest of the open house was a resounding success, and many guests expressed how impressed they were by the presentation and were interested in supporting Diversity Dawn Academy or seeking guidance on replicating the program in their own schools.

At the end of the night when all the guests had left and the students and educators had finished cleaning up after the event, Benjamin and Sarah stayed behind to lock up the community center and double-check that nothing had been left behind.

As the loud click of the door locking echoed into the surprisingly warm winter air, Benjamin and Sarah smiled warmly at each other through their winter gear. They walked to their cars together in comfortable silence, and Benjamin knew they were both reminiscing on the successful event that they had just experienced.

"I can't believe how much they've grown in such a short period of time," Sarah said as the snow crunched under her boots. "Even Brody made a speech about how beneficial Diversity Dawn Academy has been for him."

Benjamin nodded with a smile. "Brody has grown the most I think, he's come a long way from the troubled kid who showed up late on purpose on the first day of class."

Sarah chuckled as she remembered that day. "It seems like so long ago that we met them, and yet it also feels like these last few months have flown by so fast."

Benjamin opened Sarah's door for her as they approached their cars. "I know what you mean. I can't believe how much has changed since Diversity Dawn Academy started its first class." *Like my feelings for you*, he wanted to say. But he knew now wasn't the time.

Sarah smiled up at him before ducking into her car. "See you Monday," she said as he gently closed the door.

"See you Monday."

Chapter 12:

Change Breeds Progress

Benjamin

News of Diversity Dawn Academy's successful open house event spread like wildfire across Ridgefield, and various members of the community found the program's name flitting off their tongues as the alternative education model was brought into the spotlight and opinions became split into clear divisions between those who favored the program and recognized its value and significance and those who feared the change it brought about.

It wasn't long before a city meeting was called to order, and Diversity Dawn Academy staff and students alike rushed to prepare for the crucial council that could turn the tides of the public opinion surrounding the program.

In response, a conservative group within the community began organizing public protests against Diversity Dawn Academy where they claimed that the progressive values of the program were threatening to undermine the traditions and culture of conventional schooling and societal norms.

The protests sent the community into an uproar, and debates on the program's feasibility and impact on their carefully woven society spread across the city like rumbling thunder that threatened to upturn Diversity Dawn Academy's newfound stability.

Benjamin and Sarah knew something had to be done to mitigate the negative effects that the protests were having on the program's favor in the community, as they needed to secure a future for Diversity Dawn

Academy and a lack of public support could sway the school board's decision at the end of the program's test pilot stage in an adverse route.

So they stayed in the staff room at Diversity Dawn Academy long after school hours ended and everyone else had gone home in an effort to brainstorm a solution to the issue that the protests had presented them with.

"Maybe we should just face them head on?" Sarah suggested after a long moment of silence had made its way between them when they felt that they had exhausted all other options.

"What do you mean?" Benjamin asked inquisitively.

"I mean we summon everyone to a town hall meeting where we invite the skeptics to discuss their doubts so that we can help reassure them of the facts and try to gently persuade them to open their hearts and change their beliefs," Sarah said, an excited gleam in her eyes as she explained her idea.

A wide grin spread across Benjamin's face as the potential impact of Sarah's proposal dawned on him. "That's a great idea, we could dispel their skepticism in front of the whole community so that everyone can have a chance to voice their concerns and hopes for the future of the program."

Sarah smiled proudly as she nodded her assent.

"I don't know what I would do without you Sarah," Benjamin said, and he had meant it to be lighthearted and fun but he surprised himself when the words came out softly and earnestly.

Sarah stole her gaze away from Benjamin and he could see the blush creeping into her cheeks so he cleared his throat to change the subject and dissipate the light tension in the air. As he did though, he wondered if she was blushing because she knew how he felt and felt the same way, or because she was embarrassed and didn't know how to tell him to back off without sabotaging their friendship.

I wonder if I'll ever know, he thought to himself forlornly as he snuck a glance at her while they worked side by side.

***

The day of the city council meeting came swiftly, but Diversity Dawn Academy and its members had taken the time to prepare for any doubt that could be thrown their way and were feeling confident that they would walk out of the meeting with even more supporters than they had walking into it.

This confidence followed their every step as the group made its way down the couple blocks that lay between Ridgefield High and the town hall, but when they turned the corner and witnessed the sheer volume of attendees pouring into the front doors they couldn't help but falter a bit in trepidation at what lay ahead.

Benjamin knew better than to back down now though, so he took a moment to rally his troops before they entered the political battlefield that lay before them.

"I know that the size of the crowd may seem daunting, but just remember that not all of them are here to dispute Diversity Dawn Academy and how beneficial it is—some of them are here to support us," he said with a smile that he hoped sent confidence soaring into the hearts of his students and fellow educators.

As they continued walking towards the building that loomed ominously ahead of them, Sarah leaned in and whispered "You didn't even need me to help you stay grounded this time." She was referring, of course, to the many many times she had been his rock when the gushing rivers of anxiety and panic barreled down on him.

He smiled down at her and whispered back, "I always need you."

That now-familiar redness appeared on Sarah's face again, but this time she didn't look away and instead stared into his eyes for a moment before shaking her head subtly with a sly smile as they approached the town hall.

The debate began before everyone could even find their seats, as some hot-headed conservative yelled out his distaste at the thought of students relying on an untested venture for something as crucial as education.

"You're right, education is a very crucial aspect when it comes to the development of informed, hopeful adolescents who feel confident and ready to tackle any hardships that their future may hold," Jamal said in response to the man. "Which is exactly why alternative education can be such a beneficial option for many students, because traditional schools can lack the support and resources that many marginalized students require in order to develop that confidence. I know this to be true because I am one of those students. As a young Black man, I couldn't find the unbiased support I needed to nurture my hidden talents and develop into the confident Black rights advocate I am today until I found solace in the open doors of Diversity Dawn Academy."

Benjamin beamed with pride as the man sat down with his mouth firmly shut, obviously stupefied that such a young person could have such a knowledgeable perspective on the topic.

The next thirty minutes were full of similar banter, with each derisive skepticism or uneducated assumption regarding alternative education being firmly but gently refuted with simple, proven facts from the supporters of Diversity Dawn Academy.

At one point a conservative even stood up in his seat and grew red in the face as he yelled belligerently about how disgusting he found some of these "marginalized" students to be, but Benjamin didn't think that his outburst had the effect he wanted on the crowd as many were shocked and appalled by his hostile nature, even if they thought they shared the same side of the debate. The tides seemed to turn in the favor of alternative education and the myriad benefits that Diversity Dawn Academy had to offer the community when Maria, Jamal, and Alex presented the same speeches that they had shown the guests at the open house just weeks before and Kaylee presented the crowd with statistical data of Diversity Dawn Academy success and proven facts, illustrating the benefits of alternative education that the community could use to flourish and prosper.

When it was all said and done and the council decided to continue supporting Diversity Dawn Academy, Benjamin believed that the city council meeting was a crucial point in the political battle that Ridgefield had undertaken since the introduction of the program, and he did indeed walk out of the town hall feeling that the alternative education program had gained even more support than it had before the meeting began. He also recognized how important it was to foster constructive communication within the community regarding the topic and was grateful that Sarah had suggested such an effective way to do so.

The feeling that Diversity Dawn Academy had an even stronger support system was backed up by the fact that Benjamin soon found out the program received a large donation from an anonymous donor following the events of the city council meeting.

When he shared the news with Sarah, her face lit up with the same elation that he knew was mirrored in his own eyes, and he smiled warmly at her.

"I'm so proud of how far we've come, I knew this program would help showcase the transformative power of alternative education," Sarah said excitedly, her eyes glazing over with pride. "Thank you for making this a reality Ben, this is a dream come true."

Benjamin's smile turned gentle as he gazed fondly down at his fellow educator. "Thank you, Sarah, for making it all possible. I couldn't have done it without you."

Chapter 13:

Our Strength Is in Our Support

Benjamin

Life at Diversity Dawn Academy slowly began to revert to its former pace as the dust settled from the aftermath of all the twists and turns that it had just navigated through on its journey of discovery.

Benjamin and Sarah started to feel more present and invested in their classes now that they weren't distracted by setbacks and traumatic events, and they noticed that their students were shining more brightly than ever before after the results of the town hall meeting.

To top it off, Maria had just recently shared the news that her grandparents had passed their test and got their Green Cards, marking the resolution of their extended legal fight to stay in California and avoid deportation.

Alex's inclusivity program at Ridgefield High also had good news, as it had led the change that propelled the school board to adopt improved policy changes surrounding anti-bullying and inclusivity measures.

Jamal's program at the local police force was flourishing as well, and he was proud to report that he had so many people showing up to his workshops that he had to seek the support of additional staff to help him handle such large turnouts.

Coupled with the fact that the city council meeting and open house had also been such resounding successes, the air at Diversity Dawn Academy became charged with the collective elation of feeling resolve in so many aspects of the program that had once dangled on the edge of uncertainty, and Benjamin could see the stability mirrored in his students' marks. He beamed with pride at every face he saw—even the faces of the new students who had joined mid-semester in light of recent events that showcased the success of Diversity Dawn Academy.

For a moment, everything felt perfectly balanced and the future of Diversity Dawn Academy looked bright and finally seemed to stabilize, but unfortunately that moment did not last long.

The tranquil peace of Diversity Dawn Academy's recent victories was shattered by the unsettling news that another budget cut had slashed the program's chances of survival once again. Concern for the future of the alternative education program rippled through not only the members but also the strong support system that now stood behind Diversity Dawn Academy, so the effect of the budget cut was not as devastating as it was last time.

Instead of faltering or worrying aimlessly about the program or even rushing to question the school board and potentially jeopardize their mission by lashing out at their ignorance, Benjamin and Sarah leapt into action to secure Diversity Dawn Academy's stability once more. Fortunately they had a lot of support to back them up, so they soon planned a community-wide fundraising campaign to help make up for the funds that they were expecting to receive from the school board.

The night of the campaign arrived quickly, and Benjamin found comfort in Sarah to calm his nerves, just like he always did.

"Thanks for being here with me Sarah, I don't know where I would be without you," he admitted with a sheepish smile as they prepared the community center to once more host an impactful event that could shape the future of Diversity Dawn Academy.

"Oh hush," she said with a warm smile as she dusted off his shirt. "You'd be just fine without me."

Benjamin looked deep into her eyes and gently grasped her hand in his. "No, I really wouldn't."

It was at that moment that he realized how close they were to each other, and how right it felt as the air between them buzzed with an electric attraction that they had both tiptoed around for so long.

Suddenly the door to the community center opened and the two educators jumped apart in surprise, not wanting their intimacy to be seen since it was frowned upon for teachers to date each other.

Beatrice smiled knowingly at the two and crossed her arms playfully. "What's going on in here?"

"Uh, nothing. We're just getting ready for the campaign tonight," Benjamin said meekly, hoping that the heat in his cheeks wasn't as obvious as it felt. Sarah nodded beside him, looking just as flustered and embarrassed.

"It's okay guys, your secret is safe with me," Beatrice said reassuringly, the teasing smile on her face widening.

"There's no secr—" Sarah began, but Beatrice cut her off with a raised hand.

"Uh-huh, sure. You two keep telling yourselves that," she said with a wink. "Now, let's actually start making sure everything is ready for tonight."

Benjamin gave Sarah a raised eyebrow, who in return only shrugged with a relieved smile and started to follow Beatrice to the other side of the room. He chuckled softly to himself before following her, shaking his head at the awkwardness of it all.

It wasn't long before people started flowing in, and the sheer volume of the community that showed up to support Diversity Dawn Academy shocked Benjamin to his core. He knew that the open house and city council meeting had swayed public opinion in a positive shift regarding alternative education, but he still wasn't expecting so many people to be ready and willing to financially support the program. It was a very pleasant and welcome surprise however, and it lifted Benjamin's spirits to the point that he felt lighter than air from the hope filling his chest that evening.

Even local media outlets showed up to cover the event, and Benjamin thanked them profusely for attending because he knew some positive media coverage was just what the program needed to bring further attention and support to Diversity Dawn Academy's doorstep.

Maria, Jamal, and Alex stepped up to the microphone to deliver speeches regarding their positive experiences with Diversity Dawn Academy, and the applause from the crowd was deafening each time they finished their presentation.

To Benjamin's surprise, the next student to prepare for a speech was none other than Brody Walsh, who had undergone a significant attitude change and was thriving just as well as any other student at Diversity Dawn Academy.

"If I'm being honest, I was not in a good way when I showed up to the first class at Diversity Dawn Academy," Brody admitted to the crowd. "I was struggling and lashing out because I felt insecure and unsupported."

A heavy silence filled the room as his words hung in the air. "I wasn't looking forward to my future because I knew I didn't have one, and I still wouldn't have one if it wasn't for the support that I found in the outstretched arms of Diversity Dawn Academy. I not only found myself and gained confidence from the teachings that have been instilled upon me in these last couple months, but I also learned what it means to be a part of something great; something that dares to embrace the new and the different, and I wanted to show my support and gratitude for all that Diversity Dawn Academy has done for me. I wasn't ready to share this speech when the open house came around and I was too scared at the city council meeting, but I'm tired of feeling scared or embarrassed for being vulnerable, because Diversity Dawn Academy has taught me that nothing good will come from pretending to be something you're not." He smiled weakly as he looked out at the crowd before taking a breath to steady his nerves.

"Without this program, I wouldn't have a new dawn to look forward to, or a community to feel like I belong in. So I'm standing here today to show my support for the program that forever changed my life." Brody's smile deepened with confidence as he finished his speech, and it only grew wider as the crowd erupted in applause.

By the time Benjamin had expected the campaign to be over, people were still making donations and the resulting amount had skyrocketed past the initial funds that they were trying to recover. Financial stability was something that the program had never experienced, they were always scrambling for cash and cutting corners where they had to in order to just keep it afloat, so the feeling of security that Benjamin felt was increased exponentially when a significant donation sent the sum over the edge of what Benjamin had even thought was possible.

The local philanthropist who made the very generous donation said that he had been moved by the program's mission and the students' advocacy, especially after hearing Brody's speech. "I was once a young man who felt like he had no future, and I wish I could have had the support that this program is offering the students of today," he had said before making the sizable donation. Benjamin and Sarah thanked the man excessively, and he had only smiled before tipping his hat and leaving the building.

"Do you know what this means?" Benjamin said excitedly to Sarah as he turned to look at her.

Her smile matched his energy as she faced him. "We can finally move out of Ridgefield High's staff room?"

Benjamin tipped his head back and laughed as the tender feelings of hope and joy washed over him. "This deserves a celebration, let's gather everyone at Diversity Dawn Academy tomorrow and tell them all the news."

Sarah nodded and they focused on finishing the campaign, but they had to admit to each other that it was really hard not to share the news right then and there.

It didn't take long for the next day to arrive though, and the two educators eagerly shared their announcement to a crowd of students, families, and supportive community members.

"I want to thank you all for coming and express our sincere gratitude to everyone who contributed to the campaign last night. After a significant amount of donations and a sizeable contribution from a donor who wishes to remain anonymous, we are pleased to announce that the future of Diversity Dawn Academy is not only secured, but the funds gathered from the campaign put us in a place to expand the program's facilities!" Benjamin said animatedly.

The crowd cheered and the echoing sound of claps filled the morning air as Diversity Dawn Academy's supporters expressed their encouragement. Benjamin turned to look at Sarah, who smiled warmly at him as they shared a look filled with hope and excitement for the future.

Chapter 14:

Three Little Words

Jamal

Kaylee was the piece of the puzzle that Jamal didn't realize he was missing until it became glaringly obvious how perfectly she fit into his life. As soon as he met her, it felt like everything started falling into place for him. She shone a brilliant light on the darkness that had enveloped him for so long and was there for him when the realization of why his mother had hidden the truth about his father hit him like a ton of bricks.

She meant everything to him, which is why he was ready to say those three little words that he had never said to anyone except his mother in his entire life.

Their six-month anniversary was coming up soon, and Jamal knew that he needed to plan something special for her so that he could use the perfect moment to tell her how much he cared for her.

He knew she loved butterflies, so he planned to take her to the butterfly sanctuary on the other side of the city and then treat her to her favorite restaurant before driving up to a hill where he knew the view over the city during sunset was breathtaking. It was there that he planned to look deep into her beautiful blue eyes, tuck a wisp of her light blonde hair behind her ear, and whisper those three words that held so much meaning.

By the time their anniversary arrived, Jamal was so nervous and excited that he couldn't stop his hands from shaking as he attempted to put his keys in the ignition of his car. He hadn't told Kaylee a thing about what he had planned for her because he wanted it to be a surprise, but now that he was on his way to pick her up he couldn't help but worry whether she'd even like the evening he was about to take her on.

His nerves made him a mess of anxious thoughts and doubts and nothing he did could calm him down until he saw her face as he pulled into her driveway and she stepped out of her front door. Jamal put his car in park and hopped up to her porch so he could say hi to her parents before they left. While he wasn't as close as he wanted to be with Kaylee's parents, they at least weren't upset that their daughter was dating a young Black man, so Jamal decided to count his blessings and told himself that he would eventually gain their favor. He planned on spending the rest of his life with this girl, so he was sure he would have plenty of time to cozy up to them.

After a brief talk with her parents about when she was supposed to be home, Kaylee rolled her eyes and tugged Jamal off the porch.

"Have fun sweetie, we love you!" her mom called after them as she leaned against the door frame.

"Thanks mom, love you guys too!"

Jamal admired the fact that she wasn't embarrassed by expressing her love to her parents because he knew some teenagers would cringe at the thought of being so open with their emotions. But as someone who grew up with a single parent who he became really close with, Jamal knew how important it was to not be afraid of saying "I love you" to your parents, and having the emotional intelligence to not shy away from vulnerability was something he had learned from his time at Diversity Dawn Academy.

Jamal opened the door for Kaylee before gently closing it and opening his own door on the driver's side. He had worked overtime for three years to pay for the Toyota Corolla he sat in, and while he sometimes doubted whether it was worth the effort when it started making strange noises, in that moment he knew he would've worked twice as much for it just so he could take Kaylee out for a date tonight.

"So where are we going?" Kaylee asked eagerly as Jamal started the engine and carefully backed out of the driveway.

"I told you, it's a surprise," Jamal said with a wink, feeling much more confident now that her presence warmed the space between them.

"You're so cheesy," she said as she rolled her eyes for the second time that day, but her smile was warm and affectionate as she glanced up at him.

"Yeah but you love it," he said, turning his head to focus back on the road.

"You keep telling yourself that," she said, and a moment of silence passed between them before they both burst out laughing.

"Seriously, where are we going?" she said, her smile still wide and bright from her laughter.

"You'll see," he said, feeling the excitement course through his veins as he thought of how ready he was to tell her what she meant to him. He stopped at a stoplight and turned to look at her, feeling the warmth of love swell in his chest as her bright blue eyes met his. The words bubbled up inside him and threatened to spill off his tongue, and he knew he should wait until tonight when they were sitting side by side in front of the sunset, but the way she looked up at him made him feel something he had never felt before and he wanted to tell her right here, right now.

"Kaylee, I—"

But he never got a chance to tell her he loved her, because in the next instant a transport truck came out of nowhere and slammed into the passenger side of Jamal's car, changing his life forever.

Benjamin

The tragic loss of Kaylee Hudson shook Diversity Dawn Academy to its very core. After all they had just surpassed to get to a point of stability, the program was brought to its knees in the anguish that followed the car accident. In times of sorrow, sometimes seeking someone to place blame on can be a kneejerk reaction, but it almost never brings resolve and in this case there was no one to blame. The driver of the transport truck had suffered from a heart attack and lost control of the vehicle after riding down a large hill that sent him barreling towards Jamal's car. He was unconscious the entire time.

It was a dark, mournful period for everyone who knew Kaylee, and Jamal—while suffering only minor injuries such as whiplash and bruising since the main impact was on the passenger's side—was wracked with the oppressive weight of guilt. According to his mother, he had withdrawn himself to the confines of his room and refused to step outside, eat, or even talk to her.

Benjamin knew that something had to be done to bring Jamal out of his depressive episode, so he began by planning a school memorial service to celebrate Kaylee's life, achievements, and the significant impact that she had on Diversity Dawn Academy.

They used Benjamin's classroom for the service since math had always been Kaylee's favorite subject—which was why they had gotten along so well from the moment she stepped into his classroom at Ridgefield High.

Benjamin and Sarah, along with other staff members at Diversity Dawn Academy, had taken the time to transform the classroom into a space of remembrance and reflection by adorning the walls with photos, projects, and artwork that Kaylee had poured her time and energy into during her time at Diversity Dawn Academy. The result offered a glimpse into the dreams and aspirations that Kaylee held close to her heart, and Benjamin's own heart was pierced with sorrow when he found out that she wanted to be a math teacher just like him.

Maria stood in front of the classroom where the teacher's desk sits, her face lined with the deep etches of sorrow that mar her young features.

"Kaylee was more than a close friend of mine, she was someone I could confide in; someone I knew I could trust because she had never let me down. She was a beautiful beacon of light that brightened any room she walked into, and I'm going to miss her more than words can express," she said, her voice breaking as she struggled to form the words. Benjamin knew she had planned to say more, but he could tell that she didn't have it in her to say anything else and he didn't blame her one bit.

Alex gave Maria a tight hug as she walked up to take her place at the front of the classroom. Maria smiled sadly at her friend and wiped her tears, and Benjamin was proud of his students for being strong enough to offer each other solace in such sorrowful times.

Alex stood in silence for a moment, her eyes glistening with unshed tears that she quickly wiped away before opening her mouth to speak.

"It's hard to believe that I'll never see her again. I only met Kaylee when we started Diversity Dawn Academy together this year, but she became such an important part of my life in such a short time that now there's an empty void in the space she used to fill. She was a great friend and someone who you could always count on, and I wish she was here right now to encourage me to write a better speech," Alex said with a choked laugh, her tears finally spilling over and sliding down her cheeks. She looked up at a picture of Kaylee smiling on the far wall of the classroom and smiled sadly. "I miss you Kaylee, and I'm glad I got the chance to meet you because you were one of the best friends I've ever had."

Jamal stood beside Maria across from Alex, and he looked like he was struggling to make his way to where she stood so he could take a moment in front of the crowd to express the deep sense of loss that Benjamin could tell was eating away at him.

Alex walked over to where Jamal was standing and she and Maria wrapped around him in a reassuring hug before gently encouraging him to walk up to the front of the classroom. He smiled weakly at them in thanks before taking a visibly shaky breath and walking over to stand in front of the crowd.

"Kaylee was..." he began, his voice trembling with the raw emotion that was pouring off of him. "Kaylee was my everything. I never knew what it felt like to be in love, I'd only written poems about the concept of it until I met her."

He took another breath, his eyes closed in pain as he struggled to form the words that Benjamin knew he wanted to say. "I loved her, and I wanted to tell her how much she meant to me but I never got a chance."

He shook his head and Benjamin could see a shift in his demeanor. "But that's not what I came here to say, I didn't come here to talk about me—I came here to celebrate Kaylee because she was the most amazing person I've ever met. She was so kind and compassionate and she always knew just what I needed to hear. She helped me through some of my darkest times, and I will always be grateful for the time I had with her." Jamal's eyes lit up as he talked about Kaylee, and Benjamin felt his heart fill with pride as he watched his student take the first step to overcoming the terrible grief that had threatened to swallow him whole.

Diversity Dawn Academy closed the memorial with a montage of pictures and videos featuring Kaylee that students all over the school had contributed to, and it tugged on the heartstrings of each and every person who watched it. It left viewers reeling from the deep sense of loss that they all felt in the absence of Kaylee's presence, but it also highlighted the brightest moments of her life and the snapshots of laughter, growth, and learning simultaneously warmed their hearts against the icy chill of sorrow.

When the video ended and Kaylee's memorial service at Diversity Dawn Academy came to a close, the attendees walked out of the portable classroom to find a large gathering of community members at their doorstep. They all tenderly offered their heartfelt condolences, and some even offered donations or asked if there was anything they could do to help.

"Thank you all for your support and sympathy, I can't tell you how much it means to have you all by our side as Diversity Dawn Academy struggles to find its feet again in the wake of such a tragic accident." He hung his head for a moment, letting his words sink in before he looked back up at the crowd and continued.

"It's hard to even consider overcoming this right now, but it's comforting to know that we have such a strong support system that will be there for us every step of the way. Diversity Dawn Academy has had to be resilient before, and as we face this tragedy we will have to be resilient again."

Sarah gently rested a hand on Benjamin's shoulder in support as she stepped beside him to address the crowd.

"We will never forget the impact that Kaylee Hudson had on this school, on our lives," she began, her voice ringing out in the crisp morning air. "As Diversity Dawn Academy co-founders, we hereby solemnly promise that we will honor her memory by creating a scholarship fund in her name. The scholarship will ensure that her legacy lives on by supporting and inspiring future students who embody the courage, determination, and compassion that she shone brightly with during her time here at Diversity Dawn Academy."

The sound of applause fills the air, but it's not the fervent kind that Diversity Dawn Academy was used to receiving. It was the kind of applause that was filled with both sorrow for the present and hope for the future.

Sarah smiled sadly at Benjamin and reached out to gently grasp his hand in hers. Benjamin squeezed gently to tell her how much her support meant to him, and she gently squeezed his hand in response. Beside them, Alex reached out to hold Maria's hand, who then gently took Jamal's hand in her own, and Benjamin felt tears well in his eyes as he watched each and every person present to support Diversity Dawn Academy and honor Kaylee's legacy joined hands in a symbol of unity and strength. Unable to wipe his tears away since his hands were gently clasped in Sarah's and Beatrice's, he let them flow freely as his heart filled with gratitude for the support that surrounded him, showcasing their commitment to move through this together and honor Kaylee's memory by remaining steadfast in their resolve to continue Diversity Dawn Academy' mission—because that's what she would want them to do.

Chapter 15:

To Further Heights

Benjamin

As the seasons ploddingly transitioned from the tender blossom of spring to the searing heat of summer, the drowning weight of Kaylee's tragic accident slowly began to lift ever so slightly from the shoulders of those who knew her. Diversity Dawn Academy's teachers and students alike grew eager for the upcoming graduation ceremony as the days grew closer to June.

Benjamin and Sarah, along with other staff members of the alternative education program, turned their focus to securing internships and partnerships with local businesses for their students so they can gain invaluable hands-on experiences that will enhance and propel their individual growth.

Now that Maria doesn't have to worry about hiding her talent with the violin because her grandparents are the proud owners of Green Cards thanks to the efforts of Diversity Dawn Academy, she successfully secured herself a seat in the local concert hall and finally allowed herself to fully explore and express her love for the instrument.

Jamal, eager to dive into work in an effort to move on from the loss that still haunted him, took an interest in a community-based organization that promoted and advocated for social justice. With Diversity Dawn Academy's help and a dedication that had no bounds, he found a position within the organization that allowed him to be involved in outreach programs.

With the continued success of her inclusivity campaign driving her to move forward in her efforts, Alex sought out a local tech startup that valued inclusivity and diversity. The campaign experience that she gained at Diversity Dawn Academy helped her seize an opportunity within the startup to work on projects that promoted LGBTQ+ prominence and acceptance.

A collective buzz of excitement travels across Ridgefield as its students secure internships and partnerships with businesses throughout the city and business owners within the community begin to recognize and praise the transformative impact of Diversity Dawn Academy.

It's the start of a new chapter for the program, and Benjamin finds himself looking forward to the challenges and victories that he knows lie ahead as it prepares to hold its very first graduation ceremony.

It was a busy day at Diversity Dawn Academy, as everyone—from staff to students to parents and community members—at the program strives to cover every last detail during the preparations for the graduation ceremony. The trio of students who have come to represent Diversity Dawn Academy most prominently, due to the significant hardships and resulting growth that they experienced, take the lead in initiating a showcase that they plan to present during the upcoming graduation ceremony, and everyone expresses their support and excitement.

The three plan to highlight the success of their personal projects during the ceremony to showcase the growth they experienced because of the positive impact that Diversity Dawn Academy had on their individual and collective lives.

Benjamin and Sarah are overwhelmed by a flurry of emotions as they prepare to draw Diversity Dawn Academy's first year to a close, and they feel closer than ever as they celebrate the growth and success of the program they poured so much effort into.

By the end of the day, the co-founders of the alternative education program that was skyrocketing to success were seated in the staff room once again, reminiscing on how much changed since that pivotal day they met and the whole thing catapulted into action.

"You know, if someone had walked up to me before I met you and told me that this is where I would be a year from now, I would not have believed them," Sarah admitted as they sat beside each other at the staff lunch table. "I wouldn't have believed that so much could've changed in such a short period of time. This program has always been a dream of mine, a dream that was always just out of reach, until you came along and helped me reach out and grab it," she said, looking deep into Benjamin's eyes.

Benjamin smiled as he gazed down at her, feeling a warmth in his chest that he wasn't ready to label just yet. "Sarah, none of this would've been possible without you. You were the one who helped me make this program a reality, and I'm so grateful that I've had you by my side every step of the way. I don't think I would've made it through that first proposal without you," he admitted with a chuckle, remembering how nervous he was that day.

Sarah let out a small chuckle of her own, clearly following his thoughts and remembering the same thing. "I'm glad I've had you with me throughout this whole process too. I don't know what I would have done without you. That week of being distant and closed off to you was horrible, worse than what I felt when I ended things with Oliver."

Benjamin started as the realization of Sarah's confession hit him. *Is she saying that I mean more to her than Oliver did?* He thought to himself, feeling the excitement blossom in his chest before he realized how wrong it was to feel excited about being more important than someone else.

Sarah elbowed him gently as if she were reading his thoughts. "Don't let it get to your head," she said with a warm chuckle.

Benjamin felt his face relax into a gentle smile, feeling comforted by her presence and the shared experiences that brought them even closer together than they were when they first met—when and were wild enough to take a project as monumental as creating their very own alternative education program.

"Thank you Sarah, for everything. I don't know what I would do without you," he said softly, gingerly lifting his hand to cup her cheek.

It was a bold move, especially for him, and he had no idea what came over him. All he knew was that he wanted to feel the soft feel of her skin under his rough fingertips as he gazed into her beautiful hazel eyes.

Sarah's eyes widened in shock and Benjamin nearly pulled away before she melted into his touch and smiled shyly up at him. Her eyes were like pools of melted honey in the afternoon sun that poured through the staff room window, and he felt entranced by them in a way that he had never felt before. This woman had changed his life in every way imaginable, and he had struggled to stifle his feelings for her for so long that they came surging up like a great wave of emotions that he couldn't bring himself to tame anymore.

He felt himself becoming magnetically drawn to her, and he gradually realized that the space between them was slowly closing. Their eyelids were just fluttering closed as they nearly acknowledged their feelings for each other in a very tangible way when the door suddenly opened and Beatrice came striding in.

"Okay, we have got to stop doing this," she said with a chuckle as Benjamin and Sarah quickly jumped apart. "I keep interrupting you guys!"

"You weren't interrupting anything," Sarah assured their fellow educator, but the pink blush that covered her face said otherwise.

"Don't worry, I'm sure you guys will get over this whole 'keeping it hidden' thing soon," Beatrice said as she crossed the room and grabbed her lunch from the staff fridge. "It's not that weird for teachers to date you know." And with that, she gave them a teasing wink before leaving them alone in the staff room again.

As soon as the door swung closed, an awkward silence filled the air between Benjamin and Sarah as Beatrice's words hung in the air. Benjamin hoped that he hadn't just made everything confusing by leaning in to kiss her before Beatrice interrupted them when all of a sudden he heard a giggle escape Sarah's lips.

The puzzled look that must've spread across his face turned her giggle into a full-on belly laugh, and it wasn't long before Benjamin felt a chuckle bubble up from his chest as he joined in on the laughter.

Her face formed into a wide grin as she gradually stopped laughing and gazed up at Benjamin from her seat beside him. Her cheeks were still red, although Benjamin wasn't sure if it was from blushing or laughing, and it made her seem all the more attractive to him. He was done trying to convince himself that he wasn't attracted to her, and something in the way she looked up at him made him think that maybe she felt the same way.

She gently rested her hand on his shoulder after standing up to leave. "I'll see you at that dinner, right?"

Right, the dinner for the Diversity Dawn Academy staff and community tonight. Benjamin had forgotten all about it. To be fair, he probably wouldn't have been able to remember his own name if someone asked him while he was as close to Sarah as he had just been a few moments ago.

"Yeah, I'll see you there," he said, hoping he didn't sound too shaken up by the feelings that were stirring inside him.

"See you there, Ben," she said with a smile that made his stomach flip. And then she walked out the door, leaving Benjamin to grapple with the surge of emotions he felt for the woman who helped him bring Diversity Dawn Academy to life.

***

Time seemed to drag by as Benjamin waited for the day to end so he could see Sarah again at the dinner, because all he could do was think about the way she had smiled at him when she left the staff room earlier that day and how close they had been to sealing their feelings with a kiss.

He was practically buzzing with anticipation when he laid eyes on her as she walked into the community center where the dinner was being held, but they were in a room full of Diversity Dawn Academy students, staff, and community members so he couldn't go up to her and talk about what had almost happened just a couple hours ago.

You need to pull yourself together, he thought to himself as he realized what an important night this was for the alternative education program that he was so dedicated to. *Now is not the time for this.* So he took a deep breath to steady himself and turned his attention to the many supporters of Diversity Dawn Academy who deserved this dinner as a show of thanks for their monumental support and commitment to the program.

As everyone sat down after selecting what they wanted from the buffet-style table on the far side of the room, Benjamin looked out at the several tables full of Diversity Dawn Academy's members and supporters and realized how grateful he was to have such a strong support system for the alternative education program that once seemed impossibly out of reach.

He stood up and gently tapped his glass to get everyone's attention before he smiled warmly at all the familiar faces before him. "Thank you all for coming tonight. It is Diversity Dawn Academy's pleasure to show our appreciation for your ongoing support during the incredibly trying times that we've struggled through this year."

He hung his head in sorrow as he let a moment of silence fill the air for the loss that still felt fresh in their hearts.

"Let this dinner symbolize the support and nurturing that you all have provided this program with as it took its first steps this year, and know in your hearts that Diversity Dawn Academy is eternally grateful for each and every one of you. The deep roots that you have helped us sow for this program will go on to touch the lives of future students next year and hopefully for years to come if—no, when—the program is approved by the school board. This upcoming graduation ceremony is an exciting time for Diversity Dawn Academy, and I'm so glad that we have this deeply interconnected community to experience it with."

Polite applause filled the air as Benjamin settled into his seat again, and Sarah's deep hazel eyes locked onto his own from where she sat beside him.

"That was a good speech," she whispered, leaning in so he could hear her over the sound of continued clapping.

"Thanks," he whispered back with a bashful smile, feeling the heat rise in his cheeks.

She chuckled quietly, probably noticing the blush that crept onto his face.

"You never know how to take a compliment," she said, smiling and shaking her head fondly.

"Only when they come from you," he admitted, leveling his gaze on her as her own cheeks turned red.

They chuckled together as they settled into their usual warm comradery and began digging into the plates full of food that sat in front of them.

The rest of the dinner went very well, and Benjamin hoped he wasn't just imagining how full and contented everyone looked as they walked out the door of the community center. Soon it was just him and Sarah left after the last of Diversity Dawn Academy staff members had finished helping them clean up and decided to head home for the night. They both hesitated to leave, not wanting to break the spell that seemed to hover between them.

"Will you go over the plans for the graduation ceremony with me again?" Sarah asked, breaking the silence.

"I'd love to," Benjamin said with a smile as he watched her pull out a folder from her bag.

"Okay, so the fact that Ridgefield News is going to cover the ceremony is huge, but if I'm being honest it's making me a little nervous because if anything goes wrong the whole city will watch it on TV and there goes the public support that we worked so hard to secure at the city council meeting," Sarah rambled as she laid out her carefully organized plans on the last table that they hadn't folded up and put into the closet yet.

Benjamin smiled tenderly and rested his hand on her shoulders, gently turning her to face him. "It's going to be fine, nothing is going to go wrong. Those students have worked so hard to graduate, and nothing can stand in their way now. Plus, they have two pretty awesome teachers in their corner if anything does go wrong," he said with a grin.

She smiled softly and met his gaze with her beautiful round doe eyes, and Benjamin suddenly noticed how close they were.

"I thought I was the one who was supposed to calm you down when you're anxious," she said with a sheepish laugh.

Benjamin chuckled as he gently withdrew his hands from their place on her shoulders. "Everyone needs reassurance sometimes, I just happen to need it more often than you do I guess," he said with a shrug.

"Well I'm just glad we have each other to lean on for reassurance sometimes," she said, and the corners of her mouth tilted up into that smile that made Benjamin's stomach feel like it was flipping in on itself, but in a good way.

"Me too," he said as he smiled back at her, feeling so grateful for the woman who changed his life for the better and uplifted him time and time again. He didn't know what he would do without her.

Chapter 16:

The Award Ceremony

Benjamin

"You won't believe the news guys," Beatrice said as she barged into the staff room where Sarah and Benjamin were enjoying lunch together.

"Is it good news?" Benjamin asked hesitantly, afraid that Diversity Dawn Academy couldn't jump over any more hurdles this close to the graduation ceremony.

Beatrice nodded animatedly and Benjamin felt himself release a breath he didn't realize he had been holding. The talented science teacher seemed oblivious to his discomfort, but Sarah placed a hand on his arm and offered him a reassuring smile that instantly brightened his mood.

"So what is it then?" Sarah asked as she looked up from her seated position at Beatrice, who was practically bouncing up and down with excitement.

"City council just announced that The Educational Excellence Awards are going to be held early this year, and apparently Diversity Dawn Academy is a novel contender!"

Benjamin watched as Sarah's jaw flopped open like cartoon characters do on TV and felt his own face go slack from shock. The Educational Excellence Awards was the most prestigious recognition of innovative educational practices that Ridgefield had ever known, and it was beyond the wildest dreams of the educators that their humble alternative education program would be considered as anything close to a potential candidate.

"You're kidding right?" Sarah asked incredulously when she finally seemed to regain control of her jaw.

"Nope," Beatrice said, shaking her head buoyantly. "They announced it on the news channel this morning."

"That's incredible, I don't even know what to say," Sarah admitted as she sank back into her chair, reeling from the excellent news that she obviously had not been expecting.

Benjamin also found himself at a loss for words as the realization of Beatrice's words sank in for him. This could mean so much for Diversity Dawn Academy. If they were to win this award then their chances of being approved by the school board would increase exponentially.

"So, what are we waiting for?" Beatrice said enthusiastically as she looked back and forth from Sarah to Benjamin. "Let's go get ready to win this award!"

Benjamin and Sarah shared a knowing look and watched the slow smiles spread across their features. Beatrice was more than just a coworker at this point; after all they had been through as a team working to keep Diversity Dawn Academy afloat, Benjamin knew that he and Sarah considered their fellow teacher as a close friend. Which was why they were so excited to take on this challenge with her.

"Let's do this."

***

The three teachers spent the next couple of weeks leading up to the award ceremony compiling a number of convincing stories showcasing their students' growth and the success that the alternative education program helped them achieve through specialized support and resources that traditional education models simply couldn't provide for them.

They worked tirelessly to prepare a compelling submission that they felt fully expressed the nurturing environment that had proved significantly beneficial for a number of students who had felt particularly hopeless before Diversity Dawn Academy offered them hope through the influential guidance of its unique education model.

The day of the ceremony arrived before they knew it, but the weeks of preparation left them feeling a little less anxious than perhaps they might have been without it.

"You nervous?" Sarah asked Benjamin as they stood outside of the town hall once again. The huge doors seemed even more daunting than they had been on the day that their students stood by their side to support and defend Diversity Dawn Academy's reputation.

"A little," Benjamin admitted, feeling comfortable enough around her to acknowledge his vulnerability.

"Me too," she said with a shaky voice as she looked up at the imposing silhouette of the sizeable town hall.

Benjamin jerked his head to face her, surprised by her answer.

"You know, this is normally when you say something super reassuring that makes me feel better," he said with a shocked smile tilting the edge of his lips.

She chuckled nervously as she turned her head to meet his gaze with a bashful smile. "Well, maybe it's your turn to make us feel less nervous."

Benjamin laughed at this and watched as Sarah grinned at him. "Alright fair enough." His face grew serious and he stared deep into Sarah's dark hazel eyes. "If anyone can do this, it's you Sarah. You have brought Diversity Dawn Academy this far by helping us overcome every struggle that's been thrown our way, and you can tackle this challenge too because you are the most capable, confident, amazing woman I have ever met."

Sarah's face grew red and she stared at the ground in an attempt to hide it. "We brought Diversity Dawn Academy this far together," she mumbled timidly. Benjamin wasn't used to seeing her so vulnerable, but he was glad that she felt comfortable enough around him to let her walls down.

He gently lifted her chin and brought her gaze up from the ground and on to his face, finding himself getting lost in the sparkle of intelligence in her eyes that had drawn him in when he first met her. "That's right, and we're going to get Diversity Dawn Academy this award together too."

He watched as the corner of her lips tilted up in a grateful smile. "Okay, you're definitely the one doing the pep talks from now on."

Benjamin threw his head back and laughed, feeling surprised by her reaction but ready to take on anything as long as she was by his side.

"Come on, let's do this," she said, straightening her back and pushing the hair out of her face as she strode confidently up to the huge doors of the old town hall.

Benjamin followed her inside and together they made their way to the grand hall where the ceremony was supposed to take place. The high vaulted ceiling and ornately decorated walls showcased the historical value of the majestic room that had served the community of Ridgefield for many years, making it a fitting place for the traditional models of education to step aside for Diversity Dawn Academy to receive the prestigious award.

And that's exactly what Benjamin knew was going to happen, because as he stepped into that hall he found himself fueled by a surge of confidence that had him floating across the colorfully embellished linoleum flooring to take a seat among the local dignitaries, teachers, community members, students, and parents who all eagerly waited the announcement of the winner. The anticipation in the air was so thick it was almost tangible, like the crowd was holding a collective breath as the award ceremony commenced.

Schools from all over the city were given a chance to convince the crowd and judges why their education model deserved the award, and when it came time for Diversity Dawn Academy's presentation Sarah and Benjamin, as the co-founders, took their place in front of the crowd.

Beatrice gave them an encouraging thumbs-up and wide-toothed grin from her front-row seat as they found their places in front of the microphone.

"Thank you for offering Diversity Dawn Academy the honor of being considered for such a prestigious accolade as the Educational Excellence Award. It certainly was not something we were expecting when we founded the program at the beginning of the school year," Benjamin began as he addressed the crowd.

"We had to face a lot of doubt and negative assumptions as we fought to give Diversity Dawn Academy a chance to showcase the benefits that we knew it would provide its students with, and the struggles didn't end once we secured a two-year pilot from Ridgefield High School. From numerous budget cuts to physical attacks on our students and a tragic car accident that stole a bright pupil from us, our humble alternative education program often felt as if the world was poised against us, but we never stopped fighting to stay afloat in the sea of hardships that we had to overcome," Sarah said as Benjamin stepped aside to let her speak into the microphone. When she finished, she made room for Benjamin to take the lead again.

"Despite the struggles our students faced, the support and guidance of Diversity Dawn Academy's specialized education system not only helped them overcome their personal challenges but also became a catapult of growth and success that helped them find hope for a future that they didn't think was possible until they joined the program."

Benjamin and Sarah continued taking turns using the microphone to present the crowd with the lesson plans and specific education methods, such as project-based learning, that helped facilitate the achievements of their students and the statistics that they were so proud of. By the time they finished, they were breathless with anticipation for the crowds' reaction, and let themselves slump in relief when the audience erupted into a fierce applause that undoubtedly demonstrated their support and approval.

There were only a few more schools left to present after them, and soon the entire audience, including those who came to support

Diversity Dawn Academy, was holding its breath as the judges prepared to announce the winner.

"It is our pleasure to announce that the winner of this year's Educational Excellence Award is..." Benjamin leaned forward in his seat as he waited for the judge to finish his sentence. "Diversity Dawn Academy!"

Sarah and Beatrice jumped up in their seats, screaming their joy and surprise, and were soon followed by the rest of the crowd as Diversity Dawn Academy received a standing ovation for receiving the award. Benjamin and Sarah walked up to the stage to collect the trophy, and Benjamin felt as if the whole thing was a dream that his mind had made up to tease him with as he and Sarah each held a handle of the large golden trophy and shook the hands of the judges, who smiled and congratulated them genuinely.

It finally hit him that the whole thing wasn't a dream and that the trophy in his hand was real as he and Sarah held it up in front of the crowd, symbolizing the pivotal moment that it represented for Diversity Dawn Academy. Benjamin felt the familiar warmth of hope swell inside him as he turned to see the ear-to-ear grin that Sarah boasted when she met his gaze. He beamed back at her, realizing that it finally seemed like the alternative education program that had struggled to keep its footing this year had a bright future ahead, a future filled with the promise of a better tomorrow.

Chapter 17:

Growth Takes Time

Benjamin

Ridgefield High School's auditorium had never looked better. The banners and student artwork that adorned the walls brightened the space with an air of festivity that was equally matched by the attendees of Diversity Dawn Academy's very first graduation program. It was a monumental occasion for the humble alternative education program, and every single person there had wide, proud grins spread across their faces.

Maria, Jamal, and Alex were sharing nervous glances and smiles as they made their way to the stage with the rest of the graduating students, and Benjamin couldn't help but notice how mature they all looked in their graduation robes. He felt tears prick his eyes as his heart filled with joy and pride from realizing how hard they had worked to get to this moment. They deserved this celebration and so much more, and he was just glad that their time at Diversity Dawn Academy had helped prepare them to seize the bright futures that awaited them after they threw those graduation caps in the air.

Benjamin stood beside Sarah in the center of the auditorium's stage, and he felt more grounded than ever with her by his side during such a joyous time of celebration. He was so grateful for the support and guidance that she had continuously offered him as they navigated the struggles of the past year together, and he knew without a doubt that he couldn't have done it without her. He smiled at her in a way that he hoped conveyed the feelings that swirled in his chest as he looked at her, and the warm, understanding smile that she offered him in return told him that she read him like an open book, just like she always did.

He turned his attention to the crowd that had just begun to settle after arriving and taking the time to find their seats. They looked eagerly back at him in a collective glance that told him they were ready for a heartwarming speech that matched the importance of the occasion. He grinned back at them as he positioned himself in front of the microphone, as if responding to the crowd's request with a humble *I'll do my best*.

"Thank you all for joining Diversity Dawn Academy today to celebrate our very first graduation ceremony!" he began, taking a moment to allow the audience a chance to express their excitement with raucous applause and assorted whoops and hollers.

"We are all very excited to announce that every single student who started this year in Grade 12 at Diversity Dawn Academy is ready to graduate today!" Sarah said as Benjamin made room for her in front of the microphone. They stood unnervingly close, but Benjamin found himself enjoying the shiver that it sent down his spine to be in such close proximity to the woman he couldn't take his mind off of. "While that may not seem like a huge achievement because that's what every school aims for, the unfortunate truth is that many students don't make it this far. Graduation rates have become increasingly concerning as each year goes by, and traditional education systems have struggled to reverse that statistic."

Sarah took a moment to let that upsetting fact settle in for the crowd before Benjamin continued her thought as if they had practiced it. They didn't need to practice speeches at this point though, they just knew what they needed to say and worked effortlessly together to effectively deliver their presentations like a well-oiled machine.

"Which is why Diversity Dawn Academy was specifically designed to tackle that pressing issue with unique alternative models that aim to actively engage each student and specialized support systems for marginalized students who find it harder to graduate than most due to the nature of their unique challenges. The result of this alternative education model has been monumental. In spite of the grueling challenges that Diversity Dawn Academy faced as a whole and the trying hardships that some students individually faced, our tight-knit support system and unique approach to tackling issues held fast and brought us through every challenge that was thrown our way."

Benjamin smiled out at the crowd as he finished his sentence before turning to face the graduating students who stood in a group on the far side of the stage, ready to receive their diplomas.

He gestured for Maria to step forward to the microphone, smiling proudly at the confidence that exuded off of her, such a stark difference from the nervous little girl who had given her first speech at the discrimination ceremony. That felt so long ago now, but it was hard for Benjamin to believe that so much had changed since that moment.

"A few of our students have prepared speeches to express the growth and achievements that they experienced this past year during their time at Diversity Dawn Academy. Here's Maria Gonzalez, let's give her a warm welcome!" Sarah said as she introduced Maria to the crowd, which was more of a formality since the majority of the audience was Diversity Dawn Academy's support system and knew her very well by now.

Maria smiled graciously at the crowd as they clapped loudly, displaying their pride for one of the students who had faced so much this year. "Thank you, I'm so glad to be here today," she began as the applause politely died down to allow her to speak. "There was a point in my life where I didn't care if I graduated or not. My grandparents were undocumented immigrants and the incessant fear of deportation that loomed over our heads with every step we took made graduation seem insignificant in comparison." She shook her head sadly as she took a moment to remember that gray time.

"But standing here today, after Diversity Dawn Academy lifted the storm cloud of fear from my life by helping my grandparents get Green Cards, I realize how much this means to me. I didn't even consider my future before I joined Diversity Dawn Academy, but this past year has helped me unveil the bright future that I wouldn't have been able to see or achieve without the support of this program."

The crowd erupted into a standing ovation as Maria stepped back from the microphone to symbolize the ending of her speech. She smiled in appreciation and gestured for Jamal to take her place in front of the crowd as she walked back to where the rest of the graduating students were standing.

"As a young Black man growing up in a community rife with racial tensions, I often struggled to find a point in striving for a future that didn't seem like it was really possible for me. Whenever I felt like I was finally getting somewhere and the tentative tendrils of hope appeared in my life, they were always crushed by the debilitating weight of racism and discrimination." He paused and hung his head as he let the weight of his words settle on the crowd.

"It wasn't until I found a flyer for Diversity Dawn Academy that I finally gained some traction and started wondering if maybe I really could have the future that always seemed out of reach. Then racism reared its ugly head again, just like it always did when I felt full of hope, and I was arrested simply because of the color of my skin. This time though, I had the support of Diversity Dawn Academy to help me conquer the negative effects of discrimination, and the program worked tirelessly to secure my release and clear my name. It was at that point that I realized my future was possible, but it wouldn't have been without Diversity Dawn Academy trailblazing a path for me. Which is what inspired me to advocate for others like me who needed guidance and protection to secure their futures. I'm standing here today because of Diversity Dawn Academy, because without the support of this alternative education program I very well might not have made it this far."

Another standing ovation greets Jamal as he finishes his speech, and he grins out at the crowd before turning and allowing Alex to take his place. Alex waits patiently for the audience to settle before beginning her own speech.

"It can be really difficult to focus on anything other than doing your best to disappear into the background when you don't feel safe in your learning environment," Alex began as she looked out at the faces in front of her. "Which is why I struggled to plan for my future, because it was hard enough for me to get through a day at Ridgefield High without being intensely bullied for identifying as LGBTQ+. There was a specific group of girls who *hated* me and took every opportunity to make my life miserable even since I came out. I always thought that it was because they were afraid of how different I was, but my time at Diversity Dawn Academy taught me to look beyond the surface and dig deeper to find meaning. Which is why I realized that these girls treated me the way they did because they couldn't stand the fact that I wasn't afraid to show who I truly was. Those girls were so insecure that my confidence to come out as bisexual triggered them to the point where they physically attacked me."

Alex's eyes glistened with tears as she remembered the moment that she was attacked on her way home from the program, but her features quickly took on the look of resolve as her inner strength shone through.

"Diversity Dawn Academy was my safe space, and it allowed me to finally have the ability to plan for my future, to realize that I was important and belonged to something bigger than any high school. After feeling the warmth and support of Diversity Dawn Academy and realizing how much I needed it, I realized that I wanted to help others like me feel safe enough to focus on their futures. Diversity Dawn Academy not only inspired me to become the person I am today, but also to help those who didn't have the blessing of being a part of this alternative education program, and for that I will always be grateful."

Alex smiled brightly at the audience as they jumped out of their seats and clapped loudly to show how inspired they were by her speech.

"And so here we are," Benjamin said to the crowd as he stepped back up to the microphone. "After all we've been through together, Diversity Dawn Academy is proud to present its graduating students with the diplomas that they worked so very hard to achieve. Here's to them!" he called out, gesturing to the students and clapping as loudly and fervently as his arms let him to show his students just how proud he was.

When the applause slowly died down again, Sarah gestured for the students to come forward one by one to receive their diplomas. Benjamin and Sarah smiled genuinely at each and every one of them as they firmly shook their hands and congratulated them excitedly.

After all the students had taken a moment to receive their diplomas, they eagerly threw their caps up into the air and every single person in the auditorium erupted into fervent applause, celebrating the students who had just taken a huge step towards a new dawn for each and every one of them.

When everyone settled and the applause died down again, Benjamin and Sarah shared an excited look as they prepared to announce the surprise that they were ready to share with the Diversity Dawn Academy community.

"We are also very eager to share the exciting news that the University of California has proposed a partnership with our very own alternative education program!" Sarah said to the audience as she bounced with excitement in front of the microphone.

"This means more scholarships that are specifically for Diversity Dawn Academy graduates!" Benjamin added eagerly, and the crowd exploded in the most excited applause that he had ever experienced.

As the celebratory applause filled the auditorium, Benjamin turned to Sarah and beamed at her as they soaked in the pure joy and hope that surrounded them. Not bothering to care who noticed anymore, they gingerly bound their hands together and shared a look that expressed all the feelings their hearts were overflowing with in that moment, without needing to say a word.

The rest of the graduation ceremony was just as energized as the beginning of it was, and Benjamin and Sarah left the auditorium feeling lighter than air as the bright future of their students filled them with joy and pride.

"I'm not ready for this night to be over yet," Sarah admitted as they arrived at the staff room and began collecting their things to leave the school.

Benjamin turned to look at her and a slow grin spread across his face. "Me neither, I'll be bouncing off the walls for hours after that ceremony. I feel like I just drank 16 cups of coffee."

Sarah threw her head back and let out a laugh that rebounded off the walls of the staff room, making Benjamin realize how much he loved the sound of her laughter.

"Do you want to go to that Italian place again?" she asked timidly. Benjamin immediately remembered the last time they went there together, on that night that everything changed between them.

"I'd love to," he said with a warm smile.

As they walked side by side to their cars, the air between them charged with an electric attraction that neither of them addressed, he realized that his feelings for Sarah had grown even deeper than he had ever felt for anyone before. The thought both scared and exhilarated him, and, coupled with the high that he was still riding from the success of the graduation ceremony, he felt alive with hope and anticipation for the bright future that he saw laid out in front of him. For the rest of the night, there was one thought that kept circling in his head as he enjoyed Sarah's presence over a quiet dinner: *I never knew I could feel this happy*.

Chapter 18:

Against the Odds

Benjamin

The following year was as much of a groundbreaking success for Diversity Dawn Academy as it was during their first year, and they faced considerably fewer challenges as the program found its feet and its support network grew even larger and more connected. As the seasons moved through their delicate dance of transition and Diversity Dawn Academy flourished under Benjamin and Sarah's caring hands, their affection for each other grew. They knew how much they meant to each other, but neither of them took the time to admit it because there was always something standing in the way.

Whether it was a new and equally challenging hardship that once again threatened to jeopardize the stability of their program or the stress of pioneering a completely unique curriculum and dealing with all the intricate difficulties that came with it, they never found the time or the courage to express their feelings to each other and bring their relationship to the next level. And so, they found themselves in a comfortable impasse, where their determination to secure a stable future for Diversity Dawn Academy took precedence over their feelings for each other. And as the school year once again drew to a close and the alternative education program boasted another impressive graduation rate, the two co-founders found themselves in a flurry of nerves as they prepared to face the school board once again.

***

Everything—all the tireless efforts and meticulous planning and late-night brainstorming sessions, all that Diversity Dawn Academy suffered through and triumphed from—all led up to this moment.

Benjamin, Sarah, and the rest of Diversity Dawn Academy staff spent weeks preparing their presentation to convince the school board that Diversity Dawn Academy deserved to fly farther than it could with just its test pilot. They poured their hearts and souls into making sure that every angle was covered and every compelling fact was included.

The two co-founders worked overtime during a strategic planning session where they wrapped up the last details and ran through the presentation over and over again in a desperate attempt to memorize every last word and perfect their speeches. The school board's decision could shatter the walls of the beautiful sanctuary that they had devoted all their time and energy (and a great deal of their hard-earned money) into over the last year. The thought of the entire program coming crashing down was just too much for Benjamin to bear, and he knew Sarah felt the same because her eyes told him so every time he gazed into them.

So they refused to focus on the possibility of their tedious efforts being all for nothing, and instead dove into doing everything they possibly could to ensure that the school board had no choice but to approve Diversity Dawn Academy and allow the program to keep running.

The last couple weeks had been grueling for both of them, and Benjamin had lost sleep worrying about the outcome of the meeting and dreading its arrival, but now that he stood waiting for the board members with sweat beading down his brow, he found himself wishing they would just show up and make the decision to put them all out of their misery.

Waiting for the outcome of such a monumental decision was the worst form of torture he had ever experienced, worse than any of the rigorous training regimes that he was forced to follow through with during his time at the Navy.

He would rather drop down and give his drill instructor 50 push-ups right here on the boardroom floor than have to go through this right now.

Beside him, Sarah seemed cool and collected as she sat in the same chair she had all those months ago when they presented their initial pitch, but she kept her eyes glued to the door where the board members would come out of soon. He admired her resolve and wished he too could maintain a steady composure, but he also knew her well enough to tell that she was just as torn up inside by the tortuous storm of anxiety as he was.

The room had not changed a bit since the last time Benjamin and Sarah had faced the board members, and the only difference from last time was the fact that it was filled with the strong, interconnected community that Diversity Dawn Academy had grown during its initial test pilot.

Benjamin knew that the alternative education program he and Sarah had worked so hard to convince this board to give a chance to in the first place had a lot to offer its students, and the world in general, but he also knew that convincing the board to continue supporting the program and allocating a proper budget was going to be their biggest challenge yet.

Which is why he felt so grateful for the swarm of people who had managed to squeeze themselves into the tiny board room so that they could stand beside Diversity Dawn Academy's co-founders with their buttons and encouraging signs as a powerful show of silent support for the alternative education program that deeply touched each and every one of their lives.

But even the unwavering crowd of supporters was starting to sport signs of nervousness as the board members continued to delay their arrival, and Benjamin did his best to not curse them silently for trying to mess with their heads like this.

Finally, after nearly 20 minutes of tense anticipation, the board members slowly began to filter into the room and gradually settled themselves into their seats. Benjamin instantly found Peter Howes' face and searched for any hint of hope that might portray the board's outlook on the situation going into the meeting, but all the progressive board member could do was offer him a weak smile that didn't exactly send sparks of confidence shooting through Benjamin's heart.

He wasn't going to let that phase him though; he was ready to give his all and make sure that he could look his students in the eyes and honestly tell them that he did everything he could to keep the program alive if this board meeting turned for the worse. *It's not going to though*, he told himself. *I'll make sure of that.*

So he held his head high as the board members addressed the co-founders and brought the meeting to a start.

"Good morning, Mr. Diamonds, Ms. Mitchell. Today is the day you've been waiting for, huh?" Evan Peters said with a sly smirk. Benjamin watched from the corner of his eye as a muscle twitched in Sarah's jaw, and he knew that she was battling with the overwhelming urge to swipe that smirk off his face. Without looking away from the board members so they wouldn't suspect what he was doing, he slowly moved his hand from where it sat on his lap under the table to on top of Sarah's own hand by her side.

She jolted imperceptibly as he did, but thankfully he seemed to be the only one to notice and she quickly interlocked their fingers so she could give him a little squeeze. He squeezed back, and all of the sudden their demeanor changed as they redirected their conscious focus to the board, as if their joined hands gave them the strength they needed to face the decision that could rip their dreams away from them.

"So let's hear it then, why do you think we should keep supporting this little program of yours?" Evan said with a sneer as he peered at them through his glasses.

Benjamin felt Sarah squeeze his hands again as he straightened in his chair and prepared to begin his speech. "Over these past two years, the students who have enrolled in Diversity Dawn Academy have thrived under the gentle encouragement of a safe space and unique lesson plans. This experience has been life-changing for them, and we have evidence to back that fact up. Three of our most memorable students from our initial year suggested we share their powerful stories to highlight the transformative power of alternative education that our program provided them with." Benjamin paused to catch the eyes of those three particular students from their place in the crowd beside him, and the supportive and encouraging smiles that shone off of their faces gave him the fuel he needed to press on.

"Maria Gonzalez was a Grade 12 student who sought out Diversity Dawn Academy during our first year because she was struggling to focus on her grades and knew she could do better within the right environment. Her home life was troubled because her grandparents were undocumented immigrants at the time of her application to Diversity Dawn Academy, and the constant fear of deportation loomed over her head wherever she went. It prevented her from excelling in her school work because she didn't want to draw any kind of attention to herself or her family. So she got mediocre grades even though she knew she could do better and she didn't play violin in the school band despite her fervent desire to do so." Benjamin smiled sadly at Maria to acknowledge her bravery and resilience for moving through such dark times.

"When she joined Diversity Dawn Academy her grades improved significantly, but it wasn't until her grandparents received a deportation notice that Maria's true colors started shining through the darkness that surrounded her at the time. With Diversity Dawn Academy by her side, she found her courage and fought for her grandparents' rights as immigrants. She initiated a fundraising campaign to help support her grandparents and spread awareness of immigrant rights. Because Diversity Dawn Academy gave her the space and resources she needed to find her courage and embrace her leadership skills, Maria's campaign successfully raised enough money to turn the tide in the legal battle surrounding her grandparents' deportation notice, and with her help they were giving permission to obtain Green Cards. Maria's journey is just one example of what students can accomplish if they're given the support and resources they need to embrace their skills and abilities."

Benjamin anxiously looked out across the drawn faces of the board members and was disappointed to notice that none of them seemed as convinced or moved as he wanted them to be. Sarah must've noticed his frustration because she gave his hand another reassuring squeeze before taking the initiative to start the next part of the speech.

"Another student who demonstrated enormous growth and resilience during his year at Diversity Dawn Academy is Jamal Robinson. Jamal is a young African American man who grew up in a neighborhood fraught with racial tensions. His love for literature and poetry was one of the only things that brought light to the darkness that he felt engulfed by, and he was over the moon when he received an email one morning saying that he had been chosen as the top candidate for the first prize of the poetry contest that he had entered at Ridgefield High. He felt like he was finally being seen and accepted, and that maybe things were looking up for him. But once they found out who he was they quickly changed their minds, and Jamal was left with a pit in his stomach that tried to convince him he was worth less than others because of his ethnicity." Fire danced in Sarah's eyes as she spoke of the injustice that Jamal had suffered through, and Benjamin felt his feelings for her grow even deeper as she pushed on, eager to convince the board members how wrong discrimination is and how impactful Diversity Dawn Academy has been for students who have had to suffer through the harsh effects of it.

"Jamal sought out the shelter of Diversity Dawn Academy because it promised a refuge for those who felt discriminated against, and he quickly flourished under the wing of the unique programs and specialized resources. Things were finally starting to look up for Jamal, but the cold, rough hands of racism weren't done holding him back just yet. One day, when Jamal was innocently walking back from school, a police officer stopped him and harassed him because of the color of his skin. When Jamal refused to accept his disrespect and simply fold under the pressure of discrimination, the officer declared that he was under arrest. For what, he wouldn't say, because the truth was that he had no reason to detain Jamal—he just wanted to punish him for being different and not groveling beneath him." Sarah paused for a moment to let her words sink in as she stared each and every board member down. Many of them turned away under the intensity of her gaze, but Evan Peters challenged it with a glare, obviously not moved by the hardships that Jamal had suffered through. Benjamin watched in admiration as the fierce educator clenched her jaw in determination before she continued her speech.

"With Diversity Dawn Academy by his side, Jamal's name was cleared and he returned back to our program with a drive to save others from the racism that had nearly snuffed out his chance for a future. Despite the way he was treated by one of their members, Jamal bravely approached the local police force and convinced them to set up workshops that encouraged fair treatment and brought light to the darkness that discrimination can spread. Diversity Dawn Academy saved Jamal from having a criminal record that could have laid waste to the future he desperately worked toward, and he's not the only student who needs saving." Sarah's powerful words hung in the air as she finished her speech, and Benjamin hoped he wasn't imagining it as he noticed a slight shift in the board members' demeanors.

Jumping at the chance to build on that shift, Benjamin plunged on and started Alex's story before any of the board members could say something to discredit Jamal's graduation journey.

"When Alex Taylor started publicly identifying as a bisexual, her school life at Ridgefield High took a terrible turn for the worst. She became the victim of serious bullying from a group of her peers who took it upon themselves to make her life miserable because she was brave enough to embrace her individuality. She did her best to ignore and avoid them as much as possible, but being in the same school made that very difficult. Her grades suffered as a result because the bullies not only distracted her from her studies but also sabotaged them in any way they could, such as flushing her notes down the toilet and turning the teachers against her. When she failed a history test because she didn't have the notes she worked so hard to make and her history teacher refused to believe her when she tried to convince him that the bullies stole her notes, she became fed up with her poor chances of success in an environment that refused to accept and support her. So she took it upon herself to find a new school; one where she could find support and truly flourish. Her search came to an end when she sought out Diversity Dawn Academy and eagerly joined in the hopes that she could escape the horrors of bullying and discrimination."

Benjamin glanced over at Alex and gave her a warm smile as he spoke to express his pride at her bravery and determination. She was a bright young woman, and he was so glad he had the chance to watch her grow and learn in Diversity Dawn Academy's supportive environment. Then he turned his gaze to the board members and his face hardened in resolve as he prepared to draw Alex's story to a close.

"But Alex found herself face to face with the group of bullies once again one day when she was walking home from school, and this time no one was around to keep them in check. Their verbal assault escalated into a full-on physical attack when Alex tried to walk away, and she was left bloody and bruised on the cold hard pavement as they fled the scene. Before she had even fully recovered from her injuries, Alex decided that something had to change and that she was done waiting around for it to happen. In a brave and daring move, she took the initiative to start an inclusivity campaign within Ridgefield High that aimed to promote acceptance and scatter the dark storm clouds of discrimination. Her campaign was such a success that she was hired by a local tech startup that sought her skills to promote inclusivity. Alex's story is one of resilience and bravery, and without the shelter of Diversity Dawn Academy and the resources it provided her to find her courage and feel accepted, she would still be dealing with the bullies who attacked her."

The board members were silent, and Benjamin could practically see the gears whirring in Evan's head as he tried to come up with a substantial response that would refute the significant positive impact that Diversity Dawn Academy had on these students' lives. But Sarah didn't give him the chance to open his shrewd mouth before she pressed on with the final part of their presentation: the official appeal for continued support.

"As you can see, Diversity Dawn Academy has been a beacon of shining light for these students who felt stuck in the darkness of discrimination and were suffering academically as a result. This alternative education program gave them the chance they needed to help them grow into the confident, capable young adults who graduated with flying colors last year. And they're not the only students who undertook a huge change during their time at Diversity Dawn Academy; students like Brody Walsh came to our program as 'troubled kids,' but we saw through that derisive label and helped them bring out their true selves by nurturing their greatest talents and validating their feelings. Our unique educational models, such as project-based learning, allowed our students to explore their capabilities and find confidence in themselves; sparking a drive for growth that was simply not present when they were enrolled in traditional education systems. In tandem, our specialized support networks and resources helped marginalized students feel supported and accepted, allowing them a chance to focus on their grades instead of worrying about the hardships that loomed over their heads. Now students like Maria, Jamal, Alex, and Brody, whose futures seemed unsure and undecided when they arrived at our doorstep, have received their diplomas and feel confident and excited to tackle the next challenges they may face as they aim to enter the workforce as empowered, informed individuals who know their worth."

"These achievements have been acknowledged by the prestigious Academic Excellence Award, which Diversity Dawn Academy was the proud winner of last year. With the indisputable evidence that we have presented you with today, we hope you can find it in your hearts to continue supporting Diversity Dawn Academy and be a part of the change and growth that the educational system needs so that our students can not only graduate but leave secondary school feeling ready to take on their next steps and grateful for the lessons they learned during high school. Will you be the ones who help facilitate that for the students who are suffering under the roof of this school? Or will you condemn them to a life without a future?"

Benjamin and Sarah leaned forward in their seats and the entire room held its breath as the anticipation for the board members' decision filled the air with an electric charge that had the hair on the back of Benjamin's neck sticking up. This decision could change everything, and the future of Diversity Dawn Academy teetered on the brink of collapse as the board members shared a number of unimpressed looks.

Benjamin's heart sank in his chest like a sack full of bricks, and he felt himself spiraling as the thought of them denying their appeal started feeling like a very real possibility. But then he felt Sarah's hand in his as she squeezed it firmly, and he knew they would make it through this together, no matter what the board members decide. Even if Diversity Dawn Academy only had two years to shine, he found himself filled with gratitude that he had that chance to offer his students the support they needed and that he was able to spend that time with Sarah at his side.

A sudden calm washed over him as he realized that no matter what happened to Diversity Dawn Academy, he wanted Sarah to be a part of his life. Even if they had to take their program somewhere else and start from scratch, he knew they could do it as long as they had each other.

With that reassuring thought on his mind, he turned his attention back to the board members, who were having a heated debate about the costs and benefits of the program.

"The program cost this school money, and we could have put that money into other, more important things," George Harrison argued.

"And can I ask what else you would propose that the board funds instead of this program? What could possibly be more important than promoting the health and well-being of marginalized students?" Sarah asked pointedly, and George's beady eyes narrowed in contempt.

"I don't have to explain that to you," he said with a huff, crossing his arms in a way that was disturbingly similar to that of a pouty child.

"Well then, I guess that makes your point rather mute. Does anyone else have concerns that they'd like to bring up?" Sarah continued, leveling her eyes on the row of board members seated in front of her.

"I agree with Harrison's point, and I don't think it's mute at all," Evan said, pointing his chin up in the air. "The fact is that this program cost the school board a considerable amount of money and I'm not sure it was the best place for that money to go."

"Well fortunately Diversity Dawn Academy received a number of donations and is more than likely to receive donations again from the same donors and new ones in the future. Also, we can set up fundraisers if we need to further lessen the financial strain on the school board." Benjamin said matter-of-factly.

"There seems to be no reason not to continue supporting Diversity Dawn Academy, don't you agree Jackson?" Peter Howes said with a proud smile as he leaned over the table to look past the rest of the board members and shoot an expectant glance at Quinn Jackson.

She smiled hesitantly back at him, clearly nervous to disagree with the rest of the board but also obviously in favor of the alternative education program that supported diversity.

After a brief pause full of nervous glances at the other board members, particularly Evan Peters as the president of the board, her mouth set in a firm line as she found her resolve and nodded her agreeance to Peter Howes.

Evan's face twisted in anger as the smile on Peter's face grew even wider. "How about you Jenkins?"

Miriam Jenkins was the most old-fashioned member of the board and Benjamin assumed that it would be difficult to convince her to vote in favor of the program, so he was surprised when she pursed her lips in thought instead of immediately objecting.

"I'm afraid I have to agree, I simply can't seem to find a reason against the proposition of continued support for this program," she finally said.

Benjamin didn't think Evan's face could get any more red at this point, and he was worried that the man would start steaming like a kettle soon.

"And you Harrison?" Peter asked slowly, as if he recognized the dangerous waters he was treading through. George Harrison was always agreeing with every word that left the president of the board's mouth, and Benjamin had never been able to find out if it was because he wanted to win Evan's favor or if he simply didn't have the wherewithal to make his own decisions.

Benjamin couldn't help but hold his breath in the hope that today would be the day he decided to beat his own path, but unfortunately it didn't seem like his day to shine.

"I, uh, I don't know," he stuttered, throwing helpless glances at Evan, who smiled gleefully at his hesitation.

"If you need any more convincing, how about we talk about graduation rates? I feel like we haven't touched upon it enough to truly express how groundbreaking this program has been in treating that issue," Sarah said confidently as he tried to catch his eye.

Harrison didn't answer and refused to meet her gaze, but Sarah decided to press on anyway. "As you know, our program has sported one hundred percent graduation rates for the last two years straight. I think we all know how desperately this high school needs that and how significant it could be for the students who need extra support in order to graduate."

Evan's face slowly became less and less red and his face untwisted as he finally started to start seeing sense. Even he couldn't deny that the plummeting graduation rates was a serious issue that needed a proper resolution, and fast.

Seizing the chance to retry his vote again during Evan's brief lapse in anger-fueled opposition, Peter raised his hand into the air. "All in favor of continuing to support the alternative education program known as Diversity Dawn Academy that boasts a one hundred percent graduation rate?"

Jackson was less hesitant as she raised her hand in the air this time, and Benjamin could tell that she was beginning to see how important it was to support the program, even if the rest of the board didn't agree.

However, this time it seemed like the board *did* agree. Miriam Jenkins raised her hand silently, her face stern and drawn, and even Harrison took a stand and raised his own hand. The only board member left was the one with the most voting power. If Evan Peters decided to vote against the other members, they wouldn't be walking out of this meeting room with the approval they needed to keep Diversity Dawn Academy up and running.

The air became so thick with tension and anticipation that Benjamin suddenly found it hard to breathe as he leaned forward in his seat, his eyes glued on the man who could bring his dreams crashing down from the stable footing he and Sarah had worked so hard to create for it.

"I do have to agree that we need the graduation rates to increase," Evan said slowly after what seemed like ages, "or otherwise our school funding will decrease," he muttered under his breath, and Benjamin didn't think he had meant for anyone to hear that.

"So we're all in favor then?" Peter asked again, his eyes focused on Evan's face as well.

"I suppose so," Evan grumbled. Benjamin could tell the president of the board wasn't happy about it, but he was going to take the win where he could get it.

Sarah jumped up from her seat with a squeal and dragged Benjamin up with her as she squeezed him tightly in a brief hug before turning to the board again.

"You won't regret this decision, I promise you! You're going to make a lot of kids really happy," she said with a grin that lit up the entire room. And even Evan seemed to smile at that.

Benjamin himself said nothing, he just stood by Sarah's side in a shocked stupor as the realization of what just happened dawned on him.

And it never would've happened if it wasn't for you, he thought to himself as he gazed over at the co-founder beside him in awe. His chest swelled with a warmth that he wasn't quite ready to address yet, but he knew it was all because of Sarah.

Chapter 19:

A Party Piece of Success

Benjamin

As Diversity Dawn Academy buckled up to prepare for its third year, and its first year on a non-trial basis, its staff members quickly realized that news of their success must have spread far and wide because they were absolutely swamped with enrollment offers.

In order to accommodate the sudden influx, Benjamin and Sarah scrambled to convince the school board to allow Diversity Dawn Academy to expand and use spaces within Ridgefield High so that they didn't have to turn down any students who requested to be a part of the now-recognized alternative education program.

It had been another tense board meeting, especially since they had barely made it through the last one and Benjamin left this one feeling utterly convinced that pulling all his teeth out would have been more pleasant, but they somehow managed to persuade the board members to increase their budget so they could hire more teachers and to move some classes around so those new teachers had classrooms to teach in. As usual, Benjamin knew he couldn't have done it without Sarah by his side, and he was so grateful that she was in his life. They celebrated their successes with more and more "dates" (although neither of them ever called them that since they were still content to keep their relationship in the comfortable familiarity that it had flourished in over the last two years) and they grew closer and closer as each day flew by.

It was a very happy time for them, and they felt confident enough together to spearhead the introduction of new initiatives for the upcoming year that aimed to enhance the unique learning experience Diversity Dawn Academy offered. These initiatives included community service events and peer mentorship programs, both finely tailored to fit each individual student. When they announced their plans to the growing Diversity Dawn Academy community, it was met with excitement and eager anticipation, and the two co-founders felt proud to know that their efforts had paid off.

They also introduced another novel experience for the students who enrolled for the program's third year; having alumni visit and offer words of encouragement, and those planning to visit included the influential names of the three students who had made such powerful waves during Diversity Dawn Academy's initial year. Jamal, Maria, and Alex were delighted to visit the program that had helped them find their wings, and they expressed how eager they were to share their stories with the program's new students.

That had been two weeks ago when Benjamin called them, and now that he was standing across from them on the stage of Ridgefield High's auditorium once again, he could tell that they weren't kidding about their enthusiasm. The three students who had changed his life just as much as he had changed theirs looked so different now, but he knew he would always see them as the talented youth who had stumbled across Diversity Dawn Academy's doorstep and brought the program to new heights.

Jamal stepped up to the podium first, he stood taller (or perhaps he simply had grown taller) since Benjamin had last seen him, and his once short-cropped brown hair had now grown out into a stylishly trimmed afro. Benjamin could tell that he was more comfortable in his own skin than he had been when he had come to Diversity Dawn Academy seeking a safe haven from the terrors of racism. He looked like he had finally shed the darkness of sorrow that had surrounded him following Kaylee's passing, and Benjamin thought happiness was a great look on him.

"Hello Diversity Dawn Academy!" he began as he flashed a brilliant smile out to the crowd. "It's so great to be here today, what a treat to see so many familiar faces and to meet all the new ones of this program! If you're enrolled to start this upcoming school year at Diversity Dawn Academy—which I'm sure most of you are since you're here watching me speak—then you're in for the experience of a lifetime. This program turned my life around, and I can say with one hundred percent surety that I would not be where I am today if I hadn't had Diversity Dawn Academy to guide me through my crazy last year of high school. Because of this program, I'm now pursuing my dream career by studying at the university that I've always wanted to get into. Diversity Dawn Academy made it all possible, and I'm sure it will do the same for you if you let it."

The crowd eagerly erupted in applause as Jamal stepped down from the podium with a smile. Maria returned his grin with a warm smile of her own as she took his place at the podium and prepared to address the crowd. She too had grown, her hair was shorter and her eyes held a sparkle of wisdom that Benjamin had only seen glimpses of as she prepared to graduate during Diversity Dawn Academy's first year. She seemed stronger; more confident, and Benjamin could tell that her time at college was turning her from the capable young woman he'd taught into the incredible adult that he'd always known she would be.

"I have to say that I'm with Jamal when it comes to seeing all these familiar faces mixed in with the bright new ones of Diversity Dawn Academy's upcoming school year—it speaks volumes to the interconnected community that this program has gathered over these last two years and I'm so grateful for my part in that community. Diversity Dawn Academy shaped me into the person I am today, and I experienced the most influential shift in my character during the time I spent there. I'm filled with so many wonderful memories as I stand on this same stage that I stood on two years ago. It was during the Winter Concert, where I finally allowed myself to be released from the shackles of fear and play my heart out to the audience that had stood before me that day. Diversity Dawn Academy was the catalyst I needed to step into my true self, and I'm so excited to see what it can do for you as the students of the future!"

The sound of excited clapping bounced off the walls of the auditorium as Maria finished her inspiring speech, and Benjamin could tell that he wasn't the only one who was eager to hear what Alex had to say as she and Maria exchanged a warm hug before the young LGBTQ+ advocate stepped up to the podium. Just like the other two alumni, Alex had grown over the last two years and seemed even more confident than she had been when she tossed her cap into the air with the rest of Diversity Dawn Academy's first group of graduates. She seemed to have embraced her identification as bisexual wholeheartedly, as her head was shaven and she wore a pantsuit that she pulled off very well. Benjamin was proud of her for accepting herself and being brave enough to show off her individuality without inhibition. He knew she had a bright future ahead of her just like the other two, and he was grateful that he had the chance to watch them grow and prosper under his guidance during their time at Diversity Dawn Academy.

"When Mr. Diamonds called me one afternoon to invite me back to Diversity Dawn Academy so I could say a few words to the new students of this upcoming year, I was over the moon. This program means so much to me; it protected me during my struggles and helped me find the confidence that I needed to overcome the darkness that surrounded me. It inspired me to advocate for others who suffered through the hardships that I did, and the campaign for inclusivity and anti-bullying that I created during my time at Diversity Dawn Academy set the stage for the life I lead today. Which is why I was so happy to be given a chance to express how influential this program was for me, because I know it can help those who desperately need it—just like it helped me."

The trio received a standing ovation as they joined hands on the stage, with people in the crowd jumping out of their seats and whooping and hollering to express the pride and excitement that Benjamin felt mirrored in his own heart. He turned to Sarah and saw that her eyes were close to overflowing from tears of joy, with a single one sliding down her perfectly sculpted face. Her smiled tenderly down at her and slowly reached out to gently wipe her tear away before pulling his hand back to his side, but she grasped it with both of her own hands and pulled him into a tight hug. He hugged her back with all the emotion that he felt coursing through him from the speeches that their former students had inspired the crowd with, and he found himself not caring who saw them interlocked in an intimate embrace. They had always focused on keeping the deeper side of their personal relationship away from the prying eyes of the public in an effort to avoid any media scandals, but the pure bliss of the moment overwhelmed any thought of suppressing their feelings for each other as they stayed locked in a tight embrace that neither of them wanted to end.

***

The success of Diversity Dawn Academy's alumni visit gained even more traction than Benjamin and Sarah had expected because they only planned to inspire the students they already had enrolled but the event reached the public and resulted in increased interest from the public and the media, which was a huge success but also meant that even more students wanted to join the program now. This threatened to make the increased budget and new teachers and classrooms irrelevant since it seemed like Benjamin and Sarah might be forced to turn down potential students despite their valiant efforts to avoid that unfortunate reality.

"Even if we could manage to somehow magically find the space and the money to accommodate all these students, I have to admit that I'm worried about how such a huge expansion might impact the sustainability of the program, and what if we lose sight of our core values with so many new teachers?" Sarah asked Benjamin one night. They had gotten in the habit of driving to and from work together, so Benjamin was driving Sarah home after a long day of fielding questions from news reporters about how they planned on addressing the influx of enrollment offers.

"I see where you're coming from," Benjamin began slowly, wanting to make sure that she knew her feelings were heard, "but if anything could bring Diversity Dawn Academy down after all its been through in these last two years, it wouldn't be a larger and stronger support system. Think about it: Expansion is a good thing—the more teachers we have, the more students we can help. And of course we're going to be very selective about who we hire to make sure they share our core values, so I'm actually excited about the idea of accepting all these new students. We just have to figure out how we can get enough funding to support such a rapid expansion."

Sarah was silent for a moment, and Benjamin found himself tearing his eyes off the road for a split second to find her staring out the window, lost in thought.

"As much I hate admitting you're right," she eventually said with a chuckle, "I can't disagree with that logic."

"I know I'm such a pain when I'm right," Benjamin teased, throwing her a lopsided grin. "But could you imagine having to turn away students who need the resources and support that Diversity Dawn Academy can provide them with?"

"I'm not going to let that happen," Sarah said firmly, and Benjamin knew better than to doubt her resolve when her voice took on that determined tone.

True to her nature, Sarah didn't break her word. She used Diversity Dawn Academy's social media influence to reach out to their followers and ask that they contribute to a crowdfunding post so the program could afford to build a new set of portable classrooms and hire even more educators. The post was a colossal success and they ended up receiving so many donations that they exceeded the amount they were hoping for.

While Benjamin and Sarah celebrated the program's latest success, the next challenge was unfortunately not as easy to fix.

After being a significant part of the program from the very beginning, Beatrice Honey had become a pillar of support as Diversity Dawn Academy's science teacher; and the news that she was leaving left the program struggling to find its footing once again.

"I can't believe that you're really leaving," Sarah said as her eyes began to glisten with unshed tears in the afternoon sunlight. After a bittersweet farewell party for Beatrice that tugged on the heartstrings of the educators who had grown so close in the last two years, the trio was standing in front of their cars as they said their final goodbyes to Diversity Dawn Academy's former science teacher.

"I know, I'm sorry. I just can't give up this opportunity in South America," Beatrice said as she hugged her friend tightly. "And besides, you guys don't need me; you've always been the ones keeping this program alive."

Benjamin shook his head sadly from where he stood beside them. "Don't be sorry, we're excited for you—truly—we're just going to miss you because we wouldn't have made it this far without your support."

Beatrice smiled warmly at them both, and now it was her turn to have tears well in her eyes. "Aww guys, I'm gonna miss you!"

She pulled Benjamin to join the hug and squeezed them both tightly before pulling away to look them both in the eyes, her face suddenly serious. "You have to promise me that you'll invite me to the wedding."

"Wha—" Benjamin sputtered, his mouth opening and closing like a fish out of water. He couldn't even finish his sentence before his cheeks started burning, and when he turned to look at Sarah her face looked just as red as his felt.

Beatrice burst out laughing as they awkwardly pulled away from the hug. "Oh come on guys, it's time to let the cat out of the bag. Everyone saw you two at the alumni ceremony anyway. So why keep trying to hide it?"

Benjamin and Sarah stared blankly at her, each just as clueless about what to say as the other. Beatrice laughed warmly again and grasped each of them by the shoulder. "Take care of each other okay? I'll come back to visit soon." And with that she smiled and waved as she hopped in her car and drove away, leaving Benjamin and Sarah to ponder the truth that resonated in her words.

***

Benjamin and Sarah tried not to think about finding a new science teacher as "replacing" Beatrice, because they knew nobody could fill the void she left when she said goodbye to the program that she helped build a foundation for. The new science teacher they hired, Henry Baldwin, was not quite as outstandingly qualified as Beatrice had been and it seemed very unlikely that they would establish such a close friendship as they had with Beatrice, but he was eager to be a part of the team and they welcomed him warmly.

Everything started clicking into place as the first day of class started flying around the corner, and Benjamin and Sarah found themselves taking a minute to appreciate the progress that their program had undertaken recently as they prepared one of the new portable classrooms for the upcoming school year.

"I can't believe we're expanding so quickly," Sarah remarked as she helped Benjamin bring in the new desks.

Benjamin nodded his agreement as he set the desk down. "I know right, I was not expecting our tiny little program to reach so many people."

"Well it's not tiny now," Sarah said with a chuckle as she stood with her hands on her hips and inspected the classroom, making sure that everything was where it should be.

Benjamin took a confident step closer to the woman who made his life's dream possible and stared down into the deep brown irises of her intelligent eyes, wondering what he did right to deserve her presence in his life.

"Thank you Sarah, for being the one to bring this tiny program to a new chapter," he said, never tearing his gaze away from her mesmerizing eyes.

They stayed like that for a long time, neither one of them wanting to break away but also not ready to take the next step and close the distance between them.

Chapter 20:

The Dawn of a New Era

Benjamin

"I'm so happy for you Ben, I think that's a great idea," Sarah said as they stood up together from the table in the staff room where they had been eating lunch. He had spent the last couple days worrying about how she would react to his announcement, but she seemed genuinely happy for him as she responded to his sudden proclamation—although he thought he saw a tinge of sadness hidden in her eyes as she smiled up at him. He wasn't sure though, it could just be all in his head.

"Thank you, I've wanted to start this journey for a long time and now I think I'm finally ready to take on this next chapter of my life—thanks to you Sarah," he said, looking deeply into her eyes and hoping to extinguish any ounce of sadness in them. The last thing he wanted to do was make her unhappy and diminish the bright beam of joy that she represented in his life.

"So which school are you planning on going to?" she asked, dropping his gaze and turning her focus to packing up her lunch.

"I'm thinking of applying to Stanford. It's always been a dream of mine to receive a doctorate from Stanford University, and I think I can really deepen my understanding of alternative education models there," Benjamin replied, hoping that her avoiding eye contact didn't mean she was thinking he was abandoning her.

"Stanford is a great school, and you're definitely dedicated and intelligent enough to have a fair chance of getting accepted," Sarah said, finally looking up at him again and attempting a smile that didn't quite reach her eyes.

"Thank you," Benjamin said earnestly, wanting to express how much her words of encouragement meant to him. "I plan on using Diversity Dawn as a case study to explore the scalability and efficacy of alternative education programs not only throughout the country but potentially even across the globe."

"That's amazing Ben, I'm sure Beatrice would be proud," Sarah said, and this time the sadness leaked into her voice. She stared down at the ground without another word, and Benjamin could tell that she was thinking about how Beatrice had just left them, only to have Benjamin leaving her too.

"Hey," he said tenderly as he stepped forward and gently lifted her chin so he could gaze into her deep brown eyes. "I want you to know that just because I'm going on this doctoral journey doesn't mean that you're not going to be a part of my life. I'm still going to be involved in Diversity Dawn Academy. It's going to be hard to commute constantly and juggle my career and my academic pursuits, but I'll make it work somehow."

She hesitated for a moment, lost in thought, and Benjamin felt his breath catch in his throat as he waited for her response. "Have you looked into online courses? It could make it a lot easier for you to keep working and still start your doctoral journey at your own pace."

Benjamin breathed a sigh of relief that he hoped wasn't too obvious as he realized that he should've known she was just trying to help and wasn't upset about his decision to pursue a doctorate.

"That's a great idea, I can't believe I didn't think of that," he answered, and an awkward silence hung in the air for a moment as he realized what he had just said made it seem like he hadn't even tried to think of a way to stay by Sarah's side at Diversity Dawn Academy.

Sarah smiled sadly before taking a step back and turning to walk away.

"Wait," he called after her, reaching out to gently grasp her hand and turn her back to him. "I don't want Diversity Dawn Academy to be the only reason I'm going to see you," he said, his words catching in his throat as he focused on not losing his nerve. She deserved to hear this.

"I want you to be a part of my life no matter what Sarah, because you mean everything to me. I didn't even want to consider the possibility of pursuing a doctorate at first because I couldn't imagine my life without you, and I don't want anything getting in between us again. When we didn't speak because I betrayed you by asking Oliver to save the program behind your back, I couldn't handle the thought of losing you; of living a life where you're not a huge part of it. It took me this long to figure out how to tell you this because I didn't want to ruin the perfect balance we have now, but I need you to know what you mean to me."

He swallowed his fear and abandoned any sense of inhibition as he prepared to say something he should've told her a long time ago. "The truth is Sarah, I want you to be a part of my life because, well, because I love you."

Sarah's eyes widened in surprise as his words hung in the air for a tense moment, their hands still interlocked from when Benjamin had stopped her from walking out the door without expressing his feelings.

A charged silence filled the room, Benjamin felt his stomach flip in on itself as panic set in. *What have I done?*

He thought that she had felt the same way as he did, but now the confidence he had in that thought shattered like a broken mirror as he breathlessly waited for her to say something, *anything*.

But she stayed frozen in place, her eyes locked on Benjamin's as she seemed to struggle to process his declaration of love for her.

"I'm sorry, I shouldn't have—" Benjamin began, planning to apologize and take it back so she didn't feel obligated to say anything she didn't mean, when suddenly she closed the space between them and pressed her lips against his in her own silent declaration of love.

Sarah pulled away and cupped her hand against his cheek, looking up at him with a face etched full of a deep, passionate love that Benjamin felt mirrored in his chest.

"I love you too."

***

"I still can not believe that The Gerard Education Foundation chose me to give this award to!" Sarah said to the crowd as she held up the prestigious Teaching Excellence Award. She had been speechless when she first found out that she had been nominated, and Benjamin couldn't be happier for her. She had worked so hard to support and nurture her students, and he was glad that she was being recognized for all her tireless efforts.

"I want to thank everyone who made this all possible, from my friends and supportive parents to the staff at Diversity Dawn Academy who keep me going every day. I couldn't have done it without you guys!" Sarah said animatedly, with a huge grin spread across her face.

"To me, this accolade not only honors my dedication to my students but also represents a turning point for broader recognition of the transformative power that alternative education can present not only students but also teachers with," she said, her tone and facial expression turning more serious.

"So here's to a better tomorrow by focusing on the students who need us today!"

The audience jumped up to honor Sarah with a standing ovation, their excitement and anticipation for the future so powerful that it was almost palpable.

Sarah walked off the podium to join Benjamin off-stage, her face bright and flushed from the beam of pride that shone off of her.

"Thank you," she said as she stood beside him and looked down at the golden award in her hand.

"What are you thanking me for?" Benjamin asked, his face drawn in a puzzled expression.

"For everything, I meant it when I said I couldn't do it without you."

Benjamin frowned in confusion for a moment before he remembered the words from her speech.

"I thought you were talking about all of Diversity Dawn Academy's staff members," he said with a chuckle.

"Well I was, but mostly you," she said, lightly bouncing her hip off his in a playful gesture.

"Well you're welcome, I'm glad I could help," Benjamin said with a genuine smile. "And don't worry, someday it will be me up there receiving an even cooler award, so don't get too cocky."

Sarah tipped her head back and laughed, the noise drawing attention to them but neither of them cared anymore. Besides, today Sarah was the star of the show, so she deserved all the attention in the world.

***

After all of the media attention that Diversity Dawn Academy had been receiving lately, Ridgefield's community began to become more and more eager to get involved with the alternative education program that was making waves in the neighborhood. Benjamin and Sarah worked closely with local businesses to explore potential partnerships that could lead to expansion opportunities. They also provided information and advice to education institutions who sought them out and wanted to replicate the program's education model, drawn in by the impressive graduation rates and long-lasting impact that was proven by Diversity Dawn Academy's alumni.

Feeling inspired by their ability to overcome all of the numerous challenges that the program had faced recently and confident because a stream of success was finally pouring their way, Benjamin and Sarah took a daring leap forward in their journey towards spreading awareness of alternative education's amazing effects on marginalized students in particular. They pulled a lot of influential strings and somehow managed to set up a national conference on alternative education, where they discussed the myriad benefits of their proven curriculum and attempted to convince educators across the country to adopt the unique education model that was working wonders for the students of Diversity Dawn Academy. It also served as a platform for educators, policymakers, and related advocates to share their success stories, proven strategies, and professional insights, and therefore proved to be a learning experience for everyone involved. All in all, the conference was a huge success and the two co-founders of Diversity Dawn Academy left it feeling empowered and inspired by the knowledge they had gained and the insights they had shared.

Still flying on the high that they both had garnered from the success of the conference, Benjamin and Sarah arranged to throw a special ceremony to celebrate the achievements of Diversity Dawn Academy's students and staff. They decided to hold the ceremony where they had held the program's first-ever event—the community center that had supported and provided for them throughout their hardships over the last couple of years.

The community center seemed so much smaller now that their members had increased so exponentially, but they still managed to fit everyone in without sacrificing space to breathe and move around. Benjamin and Sarah stood on the stage in front of the crowd seated before them, feeling a little shocked to see just how many people now represented Diversity Dawn Academy, as it was their first time seeing them all in one place after the new students enrolled.

"Thank you all for coming today," Benjamin said into the microphone as he beamed out at the crowd. "We are so happy that we have every single one of you here to celebrate our successes with. After all that this program has been through, I can't deny that it's been really nice to experience so many accomplishments lately without as many setbacks as we usually face."

He paused for a second to knock his fist against the wood of the podium he stood on. "Just making sure that little statement doesn't come back to haunt me," he said with a goofy grin, and scattered chuckles sounded out across the audience.

"With that being said, let's take the time to seize today and celebrate the successes that have brought us together!" Sarah called out to the crowd, her smile genuine and full of excitement.

They all spent the rest of the evening enjoying the buffet dinner that Benjamin and Sarah had hired caterers to prepare for them all, and everyone had a great time. Diversity Dawn Academy's band took the stage and played a few of their latest projects and they all clapped and cheered their encouragement. The air was filled with joy and laughter, and Benjamin felt glad he was there to soak it all in.

When they had all eaten until they couldn't think of eating another bite because they were so stuffed, Benjamin and Sarah led the group outside to watch the sunset from the school's courtyard, which thankfully was nearby because no one really felt like walking too far after all that food.

The group sat on the freshly mowed green grass of the courtyard and eagerly discussed their excitement for the endless possibilities that they knew the future could hold, not only for Diversity Dawn Academy but also for each of them personally. A strong sense of resilience, hope, and anticipation for the future filled the air and united the group, leaving them feeling eager for the journey that lay ahead for Diversity Dawn Academy. They had all been through so much together, and even the newer members felt like they belonged in the program that was so welcoming and inclusive.

As the hazy California sun dipped over the horizon, setting the group awash in its warm glow, Benjamin and Sarah found themselves holding hands as they shared a look that expressed all the feelings they didn't have to say to communicate, knowing that everything would be okay as long as they had each other.

Looking out across the smiling group that made up Diversity Dawn Academy, Benjamin was filled with gratitude for the fact that they had avoided Sarah's prediction of losing their morals during the expansion, and he was grateful that their program was full of so many good people. He knew that this interconnected community was going to change the world and, in a sense, it already had.

Diversity Dawn Academy's Mission Statement

At Diversity Dawn Academy, we are committed to fostering an educational environment that celebrates diversity, encourages inclusion, and ensures equity for every student. Our mission is to empower learners from all backgrounds to reach their fullest potential through a curriculum that respects and reflects their identities. We strive to nurture a community where each individual's unique experiences and perspectives are valued and where every student has the tools and support necessary to thrive academically, socially, and personally. At Diversity Dawn Academy, we believe that embracing our differences enriches learning and inspires a more compassionate and equitable world.

Making a Difference

"A teacher affects eternity; he can never tell where his influence stops."

– Henry Adams

In a survey conducted by OnePoll in 2019, 83% of respondents said that they could recall a teacher who had made a meaningful impact on their life. I can certainly remember teachers who profoundly impacted me, and one, in particular, inspired me to go into teaching.

As teachers, we all want to make a difference to our students and hope to be remembered long after children move on… That, after all, is why you're reading this book – you want to do everything you can to make a positive difference to the kids you teach and help them understand the concepts they struggle with.

And the beauty of teaching in the modern world is that it's easy for us to share information and experiences, making a difference not just to the children we teach but to each other as teachers.

So, I'd like to take this opportunity to ask you a small favor.

With just a few minutes of your time, you can help me assist more teachers desperately trying to reach those students who have given up on learning.

Whether you are a veteran teacher looking to transition into a teacher leadership role or starting as a teacher looking for inspiration, this book is the perfect book to help teachers grow and become better educators.

By leaving a review of this book on Amazon, you'll help improve other teachers looking to transition into a teacher leadership role or inspire those thinking about responding to the hidden voice calling them to become teachers.

B0D433TLPM

By letting other readers know how this book has helped you and what they can expect to find inside, you'll show them where they can find the guidance they need to help the students who struggle the most.

Thank you for your support. We all want to be that one teacher that someone remembers years down the line – and when we share our resources, we can help each other get there. You can use this link:

Or Scan the QR Code to complete a review! https://qrco.de/bf3f7K

or https://www.amazon.com/review/create-review/?asin=B0D433TLPM

Add Me to Your Mailing list for a Free Copy of my next Book.

www.ingramcontent.com/pod-product-compliance
Lightning Source LLC
LaVergne TN
LVHW021821060526
838201LV00058B/3470